"I immediately went to my nurse manager after I failed the NCLEX® and she referred me to ATI. I was able to discover the areas I was weak in, and focused on those areas in the review modules and online assessments.

I was much more prepared the second time around!"

Terim Richards
Nursing student

Danielle Platt

Nurse Manager • Children's Mercy Hospital • Kansas City, MO

"The year our hospital did not use the ATI program, we experienced a 15% decrease in the NCLEX® pass rates. We reinstated the ATI program the following year and had a 90% success rate."

"As a manager, I have witnessed graduate nurses fail the NCLEX® and the devastating effects it has on their morale. Once the nurses started using ATI, it was amazing to see the confidence they had in themselves and their ability to go forward and take the NCLEX® exam."

Mary Moss

Associate Dean of Nursing - Service and Health Division • Mid-State Technical College • Wisconsin Rapids, WI

"I like that ATI lets students know what to expect from the NCLEX®, helps them plan their study time and tells them what to do in the days and weeks before the exam. It is different from most of the NCLEX® review books on the market."

Editor

Jeanne Wissmann, PhD, RN, CNE
Director Nursing Curriculum and Educational Services
Assessment Technologies Institute®, LLC

Associate Editors

Audrey Knippa, MS, MPH, RN, CNE
Curriculum Project Coordinator

Karin K. Roberts, PhD, RN
Consulting Associate Editor

Derek Prater, MS Journalism
Product Developer

Copyright Notice

Important Notice to the Reader of this Publication

Preface

Overview

The overall goal of this Assessment Technologies Institute®, LLC (ATI) Content Mastery Series module is to provide nursing students with an additional resource for the focused review of "Leadership and Management" content relevant to NCLEX® preparation and entry level nursing practice. Content within this review module is provided in a key point plus rationale format in order to focus recall and application of relevant content. Unit and chapter selections are reflective of the leadership and management nursing-relevant content categories and explanations of the NCLEX® test plans, the ATI "Leadership and Management" assessment test plans, and standard nursing curricular content. Each chapter begins with an overview of some of the topic-relevant nursing activities outlined by the NCLEX® test plans in an effort to guide the learner's review and application of chapter content.

Contributors

ATI would like to extend appreciation to the nurse educators and nurse specialists who contributed content for this review module. The names of contributors are noted in the chapter bylines. We would also like to thank those talented individuals who reviewed, edited, and developed this module. In the summer and fall of 2005, two focus groups of committed nurse educators gave invaluable input and feedback regarding the format and purposes of review modules. Their input and ideas were instrumental to the development of this review module, and we are very appreciative. Additionally, we would like to recognize and extend appreciation to the multiple nursing students and educators who have contacted us in the past year with comments and ideas regarding the content of this review module. And finally, we want to recognize and express appreciation to all of the contributors, reviewers, production developers, and editors of previous editions of this Content Mastery Series module.

Suggestions for Effective Utilization

Δ   Understanding the organizational framework of this review module will facilitate focused review. Each unit focuses on a specific aspect of leadership and management in nursing. Unit 1 focuses on the nurse's role as client and staff advocate; unit 2 focuses on the nurse as provider of client care; unit 3 focuses on the nurse as supervisor of client care; and unit 4 focuses on the nurse as collaborator/planner of client care.

Δ   Some suggested uses of this review module include:

- As a review of NCLEX® relevant nursing leadership and management content in developing and assessing your readiness for the NCLEX®.

- As a focused review resource based on the results of an ATI "Leadership and Management" or "Comprehensive Predictor" assessment. "Topics to Review" identified upon completion of these assessments can be used to focus your efforts to a review of content within specific chapter(s) of this review module. For example, an identified "Topic to Review" of "Prioritizing Client Care: Prioritization Principles" suggests that a review of chapter 6, "Prioritizing Client Care," and completion of the application exercises at the end of the chapter would be helpful.

Δ   To foster long-term recall and development of an ability to apply knowledge to a variety of situations, learners are encouraged to take a comprehensive approach to topic review. Using this review module along with other resources (class notes, course textbooks, nursing reference texts, instructors, ATI DVD series), consider addressing questions for each aspect of leadership and management.

- For **role as client and staff advocate**, ask questions such as:

    ◊   Who makes up the interdisciplinary team?

    ◊   How does the nurse interact with the members of the interdisciplinary team?

    ◊   How is the nursing process used in the delivery of nursing care?

◊ What are some of the legal and ethical responsibilities of the nurse?

◊ How can the nurse protect the client's rights?

- For **provider of care**, ask questions such as:

  ◊ What responsibilities does the nurse have for resource management?

  ◊ How does the nurse ensure safe use of equipment?

  ◊ How can the nurse decrease the risk of injury?

  ◊ What prioritization principles and frameworks can be used to guide nursing practice?

- For **supervisor of care**, ask questions such as:

  ◊ What factors affect delegation of care?

  ◊ What guidelines should be used when care is delegated?

  ◊ What types of conflicts are likely to arise in the health care setting?

  ◊ What is the nurse's responsibility toward conflict resolution?

  ◊ Who is responsible for performance improvement?

  ◊ What strategies can be used to effectively manage time in the health care setting?

- For **collaborator/planner of client care**, ask questions such as:

  ◊ What planning is necessary to be prepared for emergencies?

  ◊ What role does the nurse play in emergency management?

  ◊ How does the nurse effectively collaborate with other members of the health care team?

  ◊ What strategies should the nurse use to promote continuity of care?

Δ   Complete application exercises at the end of each chapter after a review of the topic. Answer questions fully and note rationales for answers. Complete exercises initially without looking for the answers within the chapter or consulting the answer key. Use these exercises as an opportunity to assess your readiness to apply knowledge. When reviewing the answer key, in addition to identifying the correct answer, examine why you missed or answered correctly each item—was it related to ability to recall, recognition of a common testing principle, or perhaps attention to key words?

Feedback

All feedback is welcome – suggestions for improvement, reports of mistakes (small or large), and testimonials of effectiveness. Please address feedback to: comments@atitesting.com

Table of Contents

Unit 1   Client and Staff Advocate

Chapter 1:   Client Advocacy, Advance Directives, and Informed Consent

Contributor: Polly Gerber Zimmermann, MS, MBA, RN, CEN, FAEN

 NCLEX® Connections:

Learning Objective: Review and apply knowledge within "**Client Advocacy, Advance Directives, and Informed Consent**" in readiness for performance of the following nursing activities as outlined by the NCLEX® test plans:

Δ   Serve as an advocate, assisting the client to identify treatment options and supporting the client's decisions regarding treatment.

Δ   Identify the client/family/significant other/staff members' needs for information regarding advance directives.

Δ   Provide the client with information regarding advance directives, and assist the client to complete advance directives as needed.

Δ   Identify what information is provided to the client when obtaining informed consent.

Δ   Determine appropriate persons to provide informed consent to the client as needed.

Δ   Determine if the client's informed consent was obtained appropriately.

 Key Points

Δ   **Client Advocacy**

• **Advocacy** is one of the most important roles of the nurse, especially when clients are unable to speak or act for themselves.

• As an advocate, nurses must ensure that clients are informed of their rights and have adequate information on which to base health care decisions.

• Nurses must be careful to "assist" clients with making health care decisions and not "direct" or "control" their decisions.

• Situations in which the nurse may need to advocate for the client or assist the client to advocate for herself include:

◊   End-of-life decisions.

◊   Access to health care.

◊ Protection of client privacy.

◊ Informed consent.

◊ Substandard practice.

Essential Components of Advocacy	
Skills	**Values**
• Risk taking • Vision • Self-confidence • Articulate communication • Assertiveness	• Caring • Autonomy • Respect • Empowerment

- **"The Patient Care Partnership"**

  ◊ The American Hospital Association (AHA) "Patients' Bill of Rights" specifies the rights of individuals in health care settings.

  ◊ The wording of these rights has recently been revised to a plain-language, multilingual document called "The Patient Care Partnership." For information about this document, go to *http://www.aha.org/aha/ issues/Communicating-With-Patients/pt-care-partnership.html*.

  ◊ The nurse should use these documents to advocate for the client.

Δ **Advance Directives**

- Advance directives are written instructions that allow a client to convey his wishes regarding medical treatment for situations when those wishes can no longer be personally communicated.

- The Patient Self-Determination Act is federal legislation enacted in 1991. It requires that all clients admitted to a health care facility be asked if they have an advance directive.

  ◊ The client without an advance directive must be given written information that outlines his rights related to health care decisions and how to formulate an advance directive.

  ◊ A health care representative should be available to help with this process. For information about the Patient Self-Determination Act, go to *http://www.ana.org/readroom/position/ethics/etsdet.htm.*

- **Living will**

  ◊ A living will allows the client to specify end-of-life decisions she does or does not sanction when unable to speak for herself. For example, the client can specify use or refusal of:

    ° Cardiopulmonary resuscitation (CPR), if cardiac or respiratory arrest occurs.

    ° Artificial nutrition through intravenous or tube feedings.

    ° Prolonged maintenance on a respirator, if unable to breathe adequately alone.

  ◊ Living wills must be specific and signed by two witnesses.

  ◊ They can minimize conflict and confusion regarding health care decisions that need to be made.

  ◊ The legal power of living wills in relation to certain life-prolonging procedures varies from state to state. The power of living wills also varies in relation to certain religious-based institutions.

    ° Some states will honor a living will only for the client who has a terminal illness.

    ° Withholding food and water from a client in a persistent vegetative state may not be legal in some states.

    ° Catholic-based facilities may not honor a living will that endorses what could be perceived as active or passive euthanasia in a client for whom a terminal state does not exist (e.g., stroke client with dysphagia who refuses placement of a feeding tube).

  ◊ Primary care providers who follow the health care directive in a living will are protected from liability.

- A **durable power of attorney for health care** (health proxy) is an individual designated to make health care decisions for a client who is unable based upon the client's living will.

- Based upon the client's advance directives, the physician writes orders for life-sustaining treatment. Examples include:

  ◊ Do not attempt resuscitation (DNR/no CPR).

  ◊ Medical interventions (e.g., comfort measures only, IV fluids but no intubation, full treatment).

  ◊ Use of antibiotics.

  ◊ Artificially administered nutrition through a tube.

- Nursing responsibilities regarding advance directives include:

  ◊ Provide written information regarding advance directives.

  ◊ Document the client's advance directive status.

  ◊ Ensure that the advance directive is current and reflective of the client's current decisions.

  ◊ Inform all members of the health care team of the client's advance directive.

Δ **Informed Consent**

- Consent is required for all treatment that is given to the client in a health care facility.

- State laws prescribe who is able to give informed consent. Laws will vary regarding age limitations and emergencies. The nurse is responsible for knowing the laws in the state of practice.

- People authorized to grant consent for another person include:

  ◊ Parent of a minor.

  ◊ Legal guardian.

  ◊ Court-specified representative by a court order.

  ◊ Spouse or closest available relative who has durable power of attorney for health care.

- The nurse must verify that consent is "informed" and witness the client sign the consent form.

- The nurse may serve as a language interpreter for the primary care provider, who is responsible for obtaining informed consent, only if allowed by facility policy and state law.

Responsibilities for Informed Consent		
The Provider	**The Client**	**The Nurse**
Obtains informed consent. To do so, the provider must give the client: • A complete description of the treatment/procedure. • A description of the professionals who will be performing and participating in the treatment. • A description of the potential harm, pain, and/or discomfort that might occur. • Options for other treatments. • The right to refuse treatment.	**Gives informed consent.** To give informed consent, the client must: • Give it voluntarily (no coercion involved). • Be competent and of legal age (otherwise an authorized person must give consent). • Receive enough information to make a decision based on an understanding of what is expected.	**Witnesses informed consent.** This means the nurse is responsible for: • Ensuring that the provider gave the client the necessary information. • Ensuring that the client understood the information and is competent to give informed consent. • Having the client sign the informed consent document. • Notifying the provider if the client has more questions or appears not to understand any of the information provided. (The provider is then responsible for giving clarification.)

Primary Reference:

Marquis, B. L., & Huston, C. J. (2006). *Leadership roles and management functions in nursing: Theory and application* (5th ed.). Philadelphia: Lippincott Williams & Wilkins.

Additional Resources:

American Academy of Family Physicians. (2006, June). Advance directives and do not resuscitate orders. *familydoctor.org*. Retrieved January 19, 2007, from http://familydoctor.org/003.xml

American Hospital Association. (2003). *The patient care partnership: Understanding expectations, rights and responsibilities*. Retrieved December 10, 2006, from http://www.aha.org/aha/issues/Communicating-With-Patients/pt-care-partnership.html

American Nurses Association. (n.d.). *Ethics and human rights position statements: Nursing and the Patient Self-Determination Acts*. Retrieved December 10, 2006, from http://www.ana.org/readroom/position/ethics/etsdet.htm

American Nurses Association Center for Ethics and Human Rights. (2001). *Code of ethics for nurses with interpretive statements*. Retrieved December 6, 2006, from http://www.nursingworld.org/ethics/code/protected_nwcoe303.htm

Caring Connections. (n.d.). *What are advance directives?* Retrieved December 6, 2006, from http://www.caringinfo.org/i4a/pages/index.cfm?pageid=3547

Oregon Health & Science University. (n.d.). *Physician orders for life-sustaining treatment program*. Retrieved January 19, 2007, from http://www.ohsu.edu/polst/index.shtml

Chapter 1: Client Advocacy, Advance Directives, and Informed Consent

Application Exercises

1. Which of the following situations are appropriate for a nurse to act as a client advocate? (Select all that apply.)

_____ Verifying that a client understands what is done during a cardiac catheterization

_____ Discussing treatment options for terminal diagnosis

_____ Informing members of the health care team that a client has DNR status

_____ Reporting that a health team member on the previous shift did not provide care as ordered

_____ Assisting a client to make a decision about his care based on the nurse's recommendations

2. Which of the following skills are integral to serving as an effective advocate? (Select all that apply.)

_____ Influence

_____ Assertiveness

_____ Self-confidence

_____ Delegation

_____ Risk taking

3. Which of the following outlines the rights of individuals in health care settings?

A. ANA Code of Ethics

B. HIPAA

C. Patient Self-Determination Act

D. Patient Care Partnership

4. A nurse reviewing a client's chart discovers that the client's DNR order has expired. The client's condition has not been stable today. The most appropriate action for the nurse to take at this time is to

A. assume that the client still wishes to be a DNR client and anticipate no action if he goes into cardiopulmonary arrest.

B. write a note on the front of the primary care provider order sheet asking that the DNR be reordered.

C. anticipate that CPR will be instituted if the client goes into cardiopulmonary arrest.

D. call the primary care provider to get the order immediately reinstated.

5. A nurse is preparing a client to undergo a total hysterectomy. The surgeon has explained the procedure. The client tells the nurse that she is glad she will no longer have periods and is thankful that "this type of hysterectomy will not throw me into menopause." In relation to informed consent, what should the nurse say to the client at this time and what additional actions should the nurse take prior to sending the client to the operating room?

Chapter 1: Client Advocacy, Advance Directives, and Informed Consent

Application Exercises Answer Key

1. Which of the following situations are appropriate for a nurse to act as a client advocate? (Select all that apply.)

  X   **Verifying that a client understands what is done during a cardiac catheterization**

       Discussing treatment options for terminal diagnosis

  X   **Informing members of the health care team that a client has DNR status**

  X   **Reporting that a health team member on the previous shift did not provide care as ordered**

       Assisting a client to make a decision about his care based on the nurse's recommendations

As an advocate, a nurse must ensure that clients are informed of their rights and have adequate information upon which to base health care decisions. Verifying that a client understands what will be done during an invasive procedure ensures that a client has made an informed decision to consent to the procedure. It is also the nurse's responsibility to ensure that staff are providing proper care and are aware that a DNR client may be a part of that care. Discussing treatment options and making recommendations for care are beyond the nurse's realm of responsibility and beyond the scope of practice.

2. Which of the following skills are integral to serving as an effective advocate? (Select all that apply.)

       Influence

  X   **Assertiveness**

  X   **Self-confidence**

       Delegation

  X   **Risk taking**

Nurses who act as client advocates often have to deal with sensitive situations that involve other health team members, primary care providers, or family members of clients. Skills consistent with handling these types of situations include assertiveness, self-confidence, and risk taking. Advocacy is not a role that is usually delegated, and influencing a person to make a decision is not appropriate or ethical beyond providing factual information and reflection.

3. Which of the following outlines the rights of individuals in health care settings?

    A. ANA Code of Ethics

    B. HIPAA

    C. Patient Self-Determination Act

    D. Patient Care Partnership

The rights of individuals in health care settings is outlined in the Patient Care Partnership, which is a document written in plain language and translated to several languages for non-English speakers. The ANA Code of Ethics provides professional standards that have been developed by the American Nurses Association for nurses in an effort to provide a set of principles to aid in ethical problem solving. HIPAA, or the Privacy Rule of the Health Insurance Portability and Accountability Act, is a law that requires nurses to protect all written and verbal communication about clients. The Patient Self-Determination Act is federal legislation that requires all clients admitted to a health care facility to be asked if they have an advance directive.

4. A nurse reviewing a client's chart discovers that the client's DNR order has expired. The client's condition has not been stable today. The most appropriate action for the nurse to take at this time is to

    A. assume that the client still wishes to be a DNR client and anticipate no action if he goes into cardiopulmonary arrest.

    B. write a note on the front of the primary care provider order sheet asking that the DNR be reordered.

    C. anticipate that CPR will be instituted if the client goes into cardiopulmonary arrest.

    D. call the primary care provider to get the order immediately reinstated.

DNR orders must be reinstated by the primary care provider on an institutionally specified basis. Without a current DNR order, the nurse must institute CPR if the client goes into cardiopulmonary arrest. Since the client has been unstable today, it would be best practice for the nurse to call the primary care provider to get a current order reinstituted.

5. A nurse is preparing a client to undergo a total hysterectomy. The surgeon has explained the procedure. The client tells the nurse that she is glad she will no longer have periods and is thankful that "this type of hysterectomy will not throw me into menopause." In relation to informed consent, what should the nurse say to the client at this time and what additional actions should the nurse take prior to sending the client to the operating room?

The nurse should ask the client to describe what the surgeon has told her will happen during the surgery. If the client reports incorrect information, the nurse should contact the surgeon and inform her that the client is not clear about the procedure to be performed. The surgeon should then discuss the procedure further with the client. The nurse should not allow the client to sign the consent form until she has been fully informed about the procedure and its subsequent implications by the surgeon.

Unit 1   **Client and Staff Advocate**

Chapter 2:   **Ethical Practice, Client Rights, Confidentiality, and Information Security**
Contributor: Polly Gerber Zimmermann, MS, MBA, RN, CEN, FAEN

NCLEX® Connections:

Learning Objective: Review and apply knowledge within "**Ethical Practice, Client Rights, Confidentiality, and Information Security**" in readiness for performance of the following nursing activities as outlined by the NCLEX® test plans:

Δ   Recognize ethical issues affecting clients, clients' health care, and the health care team, and identify when nursing interventions are necessary to promote ethical practice.

Δ   Evaluate effectiveness of interventions used to promote ethical practice.

Δ   Assess the client's understanding of his rights and offer explanations when necessary (e.g., advance directives, refusal of treatment, privacy).

Δ   Support the client's decision to refuse treatments.

Δ   Plan and provide care to ensure the client's rights are respected.

Δ   Ensure the confidentiality and security of client information according to federal and facility regulations.

Δ   Assess the client/family/significant other/staff members' level of knowledge regarding confidentiality and provide information as appropriate.

Δ   Plan and provide care to ensure that the client's confidentiality and privacy are maintained.

Δ   Recognize breaches (or potential risks for breaches) in the client's confidentiality and intervene as necessary.

Δ   Evaluate the effectiveness of nursing interventions used to maintain client confidentiality.

 Key Points

Δ   **Ethical Practice**

- **Ethics** is the determination of what is right and wrong. It is based on a system of values and beliefs that influence personal conduct.

- **Applied ethics** is the application of ethical theory to ethical problems.

- **Ethical theory** examines the different philosophies, systems, ideas, and principles used to make judgments about what is right and wrong and good and bad. For example:

  ◊ A person who believes that life is sacred may not be able to sanction the removal of life support services on a client with a severe head injury.

  ◊ A person who believes that life begins at conception may not support the use of birth control methods that prevent implantation (intrauterine devices, morning after pill).

- **Ethical dilemmas** occur when the choices available include only undesirable alternatives.

- **Ethical decision making** is the use of a systematic approach that enhances decision making and subsequent satisfaction with the decision.

The Nurse's Role in Ethical Decision Making	
Nurse's Role	**Examples**
An agent for the client facing an ethical decision	• Caring for an adolescent client who has to decide whether or not to undergo an abortion even though her parents believe it is wrong • Discussing options with a parent who has to decide whether or not to consent to a blood transfusion for a child when their religion prohibits such treatment
A decision maker in regard to nursing practice	• Assigning staff nurses a higher client load than recommended because administration has cut the number of nurses per shift • Witnessing a surgeon discuss only surgical options with a client without informing the client about more conservative measures available

- Ethical decisions can be made using the following steps

  ◊ Identification of the ethical problem.

  ◊ Analysis of the causes and consequences of the problem.

  ◊ Identification of possible solutions.

  ◊ Evaluation of each solution in relation to acceptable and unacceptable consequences.

  ◊ Selection of the perceived appropriate solution.

  ◊ Implementation of the solution.

- The **ANA Code of Ethics** are the professional standards that have been developed by the American Nurses Association for nurses in an effort to provide a set of principles to aid in ethical problem solving. For information about the ANA Code of Ethics, go to *http://nursingworld.org/ethics/chcode.htm*.

- Tenacious or complex ethical issues may need to be dealt with by a hospital's ethics committee.

Δ **Client Rights**

- The client using the services of a health care institution retains her rights as an individual and citizen of the United States.

- The nurse must ensure that clients understand their rights. The nurse must also protect the client during nursing care.

- In accordance with the Patient Care Partnership, the nurse should respect the client's decisions and avoid passing judgment in instances such as the client's refusal of care. (*Refer to chapter 1, Client Advocacy, Advance Directives, and Informed Consent.*)

- Residents in nursing facilities that participate in Medicare programs similarly retain "Resident Rights" under statutes that govern their operation.

Δ **Confidentiality**

- Clients have the right to privacy and confidentiality in relation to their health care information and medical recommendations.

- Nurses who disclose client information to an unauthorized person can be liable for invasion of privacy, defamation, or slander.

- The Privacy Rule of the Health Insurance Portability and Accountability Act (HIPAA) requires that the nurse protect all written and verbal communication about clients. Components of the privacy rule include:

  ◊ Only health care team members directly responsible for the client's care should be allowed access to the client's records. The client has the right to review his medical record and request information as necessary for understanding.

  ◊ No part of the client chart can be copied except for authorized exchange of documents between health care institutions, for example:

    ° Transfer from a hospital to an extended care facility.

    ° Exchange of documents between a general practitioner and a specialist under consult.

  ◊ Client information may not be disclosed to unauthorized individuals/family members who request it or individuals who call on the phone.

    ° Many hospitals use a code system in which information is only disclosed to individuals who can provide the code.

    ° The nurse should ask any individual inquiring about a client's status for the code and disclose information only when an individual can give the code.

  ◊ Communication about a client should only take place in a private setting. The practice of "walking rounds," where other clients and visitors can hear what is being said, is no longer sanctioned.

  ◊ Using public display boards to list client names and diagnoses is restricted.

Δ **Information Security**

- Hospital information systems (HIS) provide a centralized electronic source for information and allow primary care providers to pull together client information from a variety of sources.

- Strategies to protect client information include:

  ◊ Using passwords for access to electronic information.

  ◊ Prohibiting the sharing of personal passwords, thus preventing unauthorized access to confidential information.

  ◊ Allowing access of information only to health team members directly involved in a client's care.

  ◊ Monitoring for breaches in electronic confidentiality and reporting infractions to appropriate officials.

  ◊ Securing placement of paper-based charts to prohibit unauthorized viewing.

Primary Reference:

Marquis, B. L., & Huston, C. J. (2006). *Leadership roles and management functions in nursing: Theory and application* (5th ed.). Philadelphia: Lippincott Williams & Wilkins.

Chapter 2: Ethical Practice, Client Rights, Confidentiality, and Information Security

Application Exercises

1. Which of the following actions places client information at risk for disclosure?

    A. Placing paper-based client charts behind the nurses' station

    B. Using a universal computer password for all staff on one unit

    C. Limiting information access to health care members directly involved in a client's care

    D. Reporting breaches in confidentiality

2. Which of the following documents is most beneficial for a nurse to use during ethical problem solving in relation to client care?

    A. Patient Care Partnership

    B. Advance directive

    C. ANA Code of Ethics

    D. Health Insurance Portability and Accountability Act (HIPAA)

3. Which of the following is an infraction of the Privacy Rules outlined by HIPAA? (Select all that apply.)

_____ Reviewing the chart of a client assigned to another nurse

_____ Making a copy of a client's most current laboratory results for the primary care provider during rounds

_____ Answering questions about a client's condition with the client's daughter

_____ Discussing a client's condition over the phone with an individual who has provided the client's information code

_____ Participating in walking rounds as long as verbal exchanges occur outside the client's room and in soft whispers

4. A 95-year-old client with COPD and diabetes mellitus is admitted to the emergency department with a fractured hip. The client and her family are trying to decide whether she should undergo hip replacement surgery or use conservative treatment. The surgeon is recommending surgery, but the family believes the client does not wish to undergo surgery and her prior health problems could create life-threatening complications. The surgeon emphasizes that the client will be an "invalid" if she doesn't have the surgery. Demonstrate application of the ethical problem-solving process to the following situation.

5. A client who is scheduled for surgery is brought to the surgical unit. The client hands the nurse the information about advance directives he received from the admitting nurse and says, "Here, I don't know why she gave me this stuff. I'm too young to worry about what life-sustaining measures I want done for me." Which of the following actions should the nurse take next?

    A. Take the papers and send them back to the admitting department with a note stating that the client does not wish to address this issue at this time.

    B. Explain to the client that you never know what can happen during surgery and he should fill the papers out "just in case."

    C. Contact a client representative to talk with the client to offer additional information about the purpose of advance directives.

    D. Document that the client has refused to complete an advance directive at this time.

Chapter 2: Ethical Practice, Client Rights, Confidentiality, and Information Security

Application Exercises Answer Key

1. Which of the following actions places client information at risk for disclosure?

   A. Placing paper-based client charts behind the nurses' station

   B. Using a universal computer password for all staff on one unit

   C. Limiting information access to health care members directly involved in a client's care

   D. Reporting breaches in confidentiality

   Access to information can be restricted by password. Therefore, it is necessary for each staff member to have his own password so that he will only have access to information regarding the clients to whom he is assigned. Placing paper-based charts behind the nurses' station will limit access. Limiting information access to health care members directly involved in a client's care protects client information. Reporting breaches in confidentiality will assist with identifying problems and finding solutions.

2. Which of the following documents is most beneficial for a nurse to use during ethical problem solving in relation to client care?

   A. Patient Care Partnership

   B. Advance directive

   C. ANA Code of Ethics

   D. Health Insurance Portability and Accountability Act (HIPAA)

   The Patient Care Partnership, advance directives, and HIPAA all have some relationship to ethical nursing care. However, the ANA Code of Ethics has been developed specifically to assist nurses in basing their ethical decisions on a set of proposed principles.

3. Which of the following is an infraction of the Privacy Rules outlined by HIPAA? (Select all that apply.)

__X__ **Reviewing the chart of a client assigned to another nurse**

__X__ **Making a copy of a client's most current laboratory results for the primary care provider during rounds**

__X__ **Answering questions about a client's condition with the client's daughter**

_____ Discussing a client's condition over the phone with an individual who has provided the client's information code

__X__ **Participating in walking rounds as long as verbal exchanges occur outside the client's room and in soft whispers**

Discussing a client's condition over the phone with an individual who has provided the client's information code is allowed by HIPAA. Many health care institutions use a code system to determine who should have access to a client's health care information. All of the other options could allow inappropriate dissemination of client information.

4. A 95-year-old client with COPD and diabetes mellitus is admitted to the emergency department with a fractured hip. The client and her family are trying to decide whether she should undergo hip replacement surgery or use conservative treatment. The surgeon is recommending surgery, but the family believes the client does not wish to undergo surgery and her prior health problems could create life-threatening complications. The surgeon emphasizes that the client will be an "invalid" if she doesn't have the surgery. Demonstrate application of the ethical problem-solving process to the following situation.

Ethical Problem	Should a 95-year-old client with chronic health issues have a complicated surgical procedure that may place her at risk for complications and possibly death?
Causes and Consequences	The surgeon is advocating the surgery, but the client and her family feel that she has had a long life and would like to avoid possible complications that could lead to death.

Possible Solutions	Evaluation of Each Solution
Request a consult from a primary care provider who is not a surgeon.	The provider would provide another perspective. And, since a decision does not need to be made immediately, another primary care provider may suggest other viable options.
Have the client transferred to another health care facility that might be more tolerant of conservative treatment.	Transporting the client to another health care institution may be expensive and uncomfortable.
Accept the advice of the surgeon since he is the expert in this situation.	Accepting the advice of the surgeon does not take into consideration the client and family's wishes that surgery should be avoided.
Selection of Perceived Appropriate Solution	A consult from a primary care provider that was not a surgeon was requested.

5. A client who is scheduled for surgery is brought to the surgical unit. The client hands the nurse the information about advance directives he received from the admitting nurse and says, "Here, I don't know why she gave me this stuff. I'm too young to worry about what life-sustaining measures I want done for me." Which of the following actions should the nurse take next?

    A. Take the papers and send them back to the admitting department with a note stating that the client does not wish to address this issue at this time.

    B. Explain to the client that you never know what can happen during surgery and he should fill the papers out "just in case."

    C. Contact a client representative to talk with the client to offer additional information about the purpose of advance directives.

    D. Document that the client has refused to complete an advance directive at this time.

It is important that the client be properly informed about the purpose of advance directives and their role in protecting his rights. While the client is not required to fill out the papers, his comments indicate he might not understand their purpose, and the nurse must advocate for him to ensure his rights are protected. The nurse, however, should never coerce a client into signing any legal forms, even if she believes it would be in the client's best interest. The client's actions should be documented, but that is not enough to ensure his rights.

Unit 1   Client and Staff Advocate

Chapter 3:   Legal Responsibilities

Contributor: Polly Gerber Zimmermann, MS, MBA, RN, CEN, FAEN

 NCLEX® Connections:

> **Learning Objective**: Review and apply knowledge within "**Legal Responsibilities**" in readiness for performance of the following nursing activities as outlined by the NCLEX® test plans:
>
> Δ Recognize legal concerns that impact the client/family/significant other during treatment.
>
> Δ Inform the client and members of the health care team about client rights, which include the client's right to treatment, the right to refuse treatment, and the right to informed consent.
>
> Δ Follow agency policies to protect the client's valuables/property.
>
> Δ Acknowledge appropriate scope of practice and actions to take when requested to practice out of scope.
>
> Δ Recognize incidents of inappropriate client care (e.g., abuse, neglect, unsafe environment, injury) and notify appropriate personnel.
>
> Δ Identify when nursing interventions are necessary to address a health care team member's unsafe practice.
>
> Δ Report communicable diseases per agency policy.
>
> Δ Demonstrate correct procedures for obtaining and transcribing verbal and telephone orders.

 Key Points

Δ **Standards of Care (Practice)**

• A nurse bases his practice on established standards of care or legal guidelines for care. These standards of care can be found in:

◊ The **nurse practice act** of each state. This act governs nursing practice, and its legal guidelines for practice are established and enforced through a state board of nursing or other government agency.

° Nurse practice acts vary from state to state, making it obligatory for the nurse to be informed about her state's nurse practice act as it defines the legal parameters of practice.

◊ Published **standards of nursing practice,** which are developed by professional organizations and specialty groups including the American Nurses Association (ANA), the American Association of Critical Care Nurses (AACN), and the American Association of Occupational Health Nurses (AAOHN).

◊ Health care facility **policies and procedures**.

° These should be readily available in a facility's policy and procedure manual, and they provide the most specific guidelines for a given situation within the nurse's facility.

- Standards of care identify the proficient level of care that should be given, and they are used in malpractice lawsuits to determine if that level was maintained.

Δ **Professional Negligence**

- Professional negligence is the failure of a person with professional training to act in a reasonable and prudent manner. The terms "reasonable and prudent" are generally used to describe a person who has the average judgment, foresight, intelligence, and skill that would be expected of a person with similar training and experience.

- The five elements necessary to prove professional negligence are:

Element of Liability	Explanation	Example: Client Who is a Fall Risk
1. Duty to provide care as defined by a standard	Care that should be given or what a reasonably prudent nurse would do	The nurse should complete a fall risk assessment for all clients upon admission, per facility protocol.
2. Breech of duty by failure to meet standard	Failure to give the standard of care that should have been given	The nurse does not perform a fall risk assessment during admission.
3. Foreseeability of harm	Knowledge that failing to give proper standard of care may cause harm to the client	The nurse should know that failure to take fall risk precautions may endanger a client at risk for falls.
4. Breech of duty has potential to cause harm (combines elements 2 and 3)	Failure to meet standard had potential to cause harm – relationship must be provable	If a fall risk assessment is not performed, the client's risk for falls is not determined and the proper precautions are not put in place.
5. Harm occurs	Actual harm to client occurs	The client falls out of bed and breaks his hip.

- The negligence issues that prompt most malpractice suits include failure to:
  - ◊ Follow either professional or facility established standards of care.
  - ◊ Use equipment in a responsible and knowledgeable manner.
  - ◊ Communicate effectively and thoroughly with the client.
  - ◊ Document care that was provided.
  - ◊ Properly assess and monitor the client according to a prescribed routine.
  - ◊ Act as a client advocate by protecting the client's rights and ensuring the proper standard of care.
- Nurses can avoid being liable for negligence by:
  - ◊ Following standards of care.
  - ◊ Giving competent care.
  - ◊ Communicating with other health team members.
  - ◊ Developing a caring rapport with clients.
  - ◊ Fully documenting assessments, interventions, and evaluations.

Follow standards of care.

Give competent care.

Communicate with other health team members.

Develop a caring rapport with clients.

Fully document assessments, interventions, and evaluations.

Δ   **Intentional and Unintentional Torts**

- Nurses can intentionally or unintentionally commit a **tort**. A tort is a legal "wrong" committed against a person or property that renders the person who committed it liable for damages.

- Assault, battery, and false imprisonment are the most frequently encountered intentional torts. Negligence is the most common unintentional tort.

Intentional Tort	Example
Assault	The conduct of one person makes another person fearful and apprehensive (e.g., threatening to place a nasogastric tube in a client who is refusing to eat).
Battery	Intentional and wrongful physical contact with a person that involves an injury or offensive contact (e.g., restraining a client and administering an injection against her wishes).
False imprisonment	A person is confined or restrained against his will (e.g., using restraints on competent client to prevent his leaving the health care facility).

Nursing Interventions

Δ   **Ensure Safe and Legal Care**

- Establish positive, caring client relationships that foster an open exchange of communication. This facilitates provision of competent, individualized care.

- Maintain and update knowledge and skills to ensure practice is current and follows set standards. This is done in an effort to meet client expectations.

- Ensure that the client understands his rights and treatment objectives.

- All health care team members should uphold policies that govern the client's personal and property rights.

- Provide an interpreter for the client who does not speak English to ensure accurate translation of interactions with health care team members.

- Allow the client who has been admitted to a health care facility the right to refuse treatment and leave against medical advice. If a client chooses to leave the facility against medical advice, the nurse must document information given to the client. Documentation includes:

    ◊   Possible complications that could occur without treatment.

    ◊   Possibility of permanent physical or mental impairment or disability.

    ◊   Possibility of other complications that could lead to death.

Δ Scope of Practice

- A nurse should refuse to practice beyond the legal scope of practice and/or outside of her area of competence regardless of reason (e.g., staffing shortage, lack of appropriate personnel).

- Clarify, with appropriate personnel, current legal scope of practice and area of competence.

- Notify the appropriate supervisor if indicated. For example:

  ◊ A nurse who typically works on a postpartum unit should not accept an assignment to work in the intensive care unit.

  ◊ A new graduate who has never put in a nasogastric tube without supervision should not attempt this procedure without being observed by an experienced nurse.

Δ Delegation

- Delegation of a nurse-related task or activity to another health care team member must take into account the five rights of delegation: right task, right circumstance, right person, right direction/communication, and right supervision/evaluation.

  ◊ The nurse may transfer the responsibility for the performance of a task or activity but **retains accountability** for its outcome.

  ◊ The **risk of liability** with delegation relates to the appropriateness of the delegation to an individual and the monitoring of the performance.

- Use informed judgment when decisions are made regarding the delegation process. (*Refer to chapter 7, Assigning, Delegating, and Supervising Client Care.*)

Δ Transcribing Medical Orders

- Use strategies to prevent errors when taking a medical order that is given verbally or over the phone by the primary care provider.

  ◊ Have a second RN (or a licensed practical nurse) listen on a phone extension.

  ◊ Repeat back the order given, making sure to include medication name (spell if necessary), dosage, time, and route.

  ◊ Document reading back the order and the presence of the second nurse on the phone extension.

  ◊ Question any order that may seem contraindicated due to a previous order or client condition.

Δ   Reporting

- Report any suspicion of abuse following facility policy. Social workers are often invited to help assess what are frequently complex relationships and environmental situations.

- Report the client who has been diagnosed with a communicable disease to the proper agency (e.g., local health department, state health department).

  ◊   A complete list of reportable diseases and a description of the reporting system are available through the Centers for Disease Control and Prevention Web site, *www.cdc.gov*. Each state mandates which diseases must be reported in that state. There are more than 60 communicable diseases that must be reported to public health departments to allow officials to:

  - Ensure appropriate medical treatment of diseases (e.g., tuberculosis).

  - Monitor for common-source outbreaks (e.g., foodborne – hepatitis A).

  - Plan and evaluate control and prevention plans (e.g., immunizations for preventable diseases).

  - Identify outbreaks and epidemics.

  - Determine public health priorities based on trends.

Primary Reference:

Marquis, B. L., & Huston, C. J. (2006). *Leadership roles and management functions in nursing: Theory and application* (5th ed.). Philadelphia: Lippincott Williams & Wilkins.

Chapter 3: Legal Responsibilities

Application Exercises

1. A client in the emergency department has been diagnosed with acute appendicitis with a recommendation for an immediate appendectomy. The client begins to put his clothes on, saying he does not want to have surgery and is going home. Which of the following is the most important action by the nurse prior to the client leaving the facility?

   A. Validate that the client understands the consequences of his decision, including the possibility of death.

   B. Obtain the client's signature on the "against medical advice" form prior to his departure.

   C. Ask security to detain him until a legally responsible person can sign the surgical permit for him.

   D. Do nothing and let him leave without incident due to his right to refuse treatment.

2. A toddler is being treated in the emergency department following a head contusion from a playground accident. History reveals the toddler lives at home with only her mother. The primary care provider's discharge instructions include waking the child up every hour during the night to assess for signs of a possible head injury. In which of the following situations should the nurse intervene and attempt to prevent discharge?

   A. The mother states she does not have insurance or money for a follow-up visit.

   B. The child states her head hurts and she wants to go home.

   C. The nurse smells alcohol on the mother's breath.

   D. The mother verbalizes fear about taking the child home and requests she be kept overnight.

3. A new graduate nurse is preparing to insert an intravenous catheter in a client. While she has done this twice in nursing school, she would feel more confident if she could review the procedure again before insertion. Which of the following sources should the nurse use to obtain this information and the standard at which it should be performed?

   A. Internet

   B. Institutional policy and procedure manual

   C. Nursing skills textbook

   D. Nurse practice act

4. Which of the following actions by a nurse can minimize her chances of being charged with negligence? (Select all that apply.)

_____ Thoroughly explaining procedures prior to performing them

_____ Approaching the client in a caring manner

_____ Asking the client if she has any questions about her care

_____ Providing care according to the plan of care

_____ Documenting assessments in the client's medical record

_____ Carrying out the primary care provider's orders without question

5. A nurse witnesses an assistive personnel (AP) under her supervision reprimanding a client for not using the urinal properly. The AP threatens to put a diaper on the client if he does not use the urinal more carefully next time. Which of the following torts is the AP committing?

A. Assault

B. Battery

C. False imprisonment

D. Invasion of privacy

6. What is the most appropriate action by a nurse who is asked to float to a unit where he does not feel educationally and experientially prepared to care for the clients?

Chapter 3: Legal Responsibilities

Application Exercises Answer Key

1. A client in the emergency department has been diagnosed with acute appendicitis with a recommendation for an immediate appendectomy. The client begins to put his clothes on, saying he does not want to have surgery and is going home. Which of the following is the most important action by the nurse prior to the client leaving the facility?

   A. **Validate that the client understands the consequences of his decision, including the possibility of death.**

   B. Obtain the client's signature on the "against medical advice" form prior to his departure.

   C. Ask security to detain him until a legally responsible person can sign the surgical permit for him.

   D. Do nothing and let him leave without incident due to his right to refuse treatment.

   Clients can refuse care at any time for any reason as long as they are not impaired (e.g., alcohol, drugs), are competent (e.g., of normal intelligence, alert, and oriented), and understand the consequences of the decision. Subsequently, the most important action by the nurse is to make sure the client understands the consequences of his actions. While clients who leave against medical advice are encouraged to sign the relevant form, it is not legally necessary. The nurse, however, should carefully and thoroughly document what information was provided to the client and his response. Asking security to detain the client could be considered false imprisonment. Letting him leave does not ensure that he is making an informed decision.

2. A toddler is being treated in the emergency department following a head contusion from a playground accident. History reveals the toddler lives at home with only her mother. The primary care provider's discharge instructions include waking the child up every hour during the night to assess for signs of a possible head injury. In which of the following situations should the nurse intervene and attempt to prevent discharge?

    A. The mother states she does not have insurance or money for a follow-up visit.

    B. The child states her head hurts and she wants to go home.

    C. The nurse smells alcohol on the mother's breath.

    D. The mother verbalizes fear about taking the child home and requests she be kept overnight.

It would be unsafe to send a child who requires hourly monitoring home with a mother who might be chemically impaired. It is the nurse's responsibility to detect possible harm and research other options, such as admission to the facility or the enlistment and aid of another family member. Lack of insurance should not contraindicate discharge, but information should be made available about agencies that can provide follow-up care based on financial need. Education regarding the hourly assessments and provision of the facility's phone number should be provided to help reduce the mother's fear about taking the child home.

3. A new graduate nurse is preparing to insert an intravenous catheter in a client. While she has done this twice in nursing school, she would feel more confident if she could review the procedure again before insertion. Which of the following sources should the nurse use to obtain this information and the standard at which it should be performed?

    A. Internet

    B. Institutional policy and procedure manual

    C. Nursing skills textbook

    D. Nurse practice act

The Internet, the institutional policy and procedure manual, and a nursing skills textbook would all provide information about the procedure, but only the policy and procedure manual will provide guidelines according to the standard set by the health care institution. The state's nurse practice act defines the legal practice of nursing. It is not specific enough to provide guidance in this situation.

4. Which of the following actions by a nurse can minimize her chances of being charged with negligence? (Select all that apply.)

__X__ Thoroughly explaining procedures prior to performing them

__X__ Approaching the client in a caring manner

__X__ Asking the client if she has any questions about her care

__X__ Providing care according to the plan of care

__X__ Documenting assessments in the client's medical record

_____ Carrying out the primary care provider's orders without question

All but the last action can help the client receive (and perceive that she is receiving) competent, caring, and thorough client care. If all these criteria are met, the chances of negligence occurring are minimized. It is necessary to question a primary care provider's order if the nurse deems it could have adverse effects on the client or if it is contraindicated secondary to another condition or treatment. If the nurse carries out an order that goes against what a reasonable and prudent nurse should know, he could be held liable for implementing the order.

5. A nurse witnesses an assistive personnel (AP) under her supervision reprimanding a client for not using the urinal properly. The AP threatens to put a diaper on the client if he does not use the urinal more carefully next time. Which of the following torts is the AP committing?

A. Assault

B. Battery

C. False imprisonment

D. Invasion of privacy

By threatening the client, the AP is committing assault. Her threats could make the client become fearful and apprehensive. Since the AP has only verbally threatened the client, battery has not occurred. False imprisonment and invasion of privacy have not been committed.

6. What is the most appropriate action by a nurse who is asked to float to a unit where he does not feel educationally and experientially prepared to care for the clients?

The nurse should explain to the assignment nurse that he does not feel qualified to provide care on that unit and that doing so could cause him to provide substandard care. The nurse should problem solve other options with the assignment nurse and/or supervisor regarding other units to which the nurse could float. If none of these options are acceptable, discuss the situation with the unit manager, who should advocate for the nurse and his concern for safe client practice.

Unit 2   Provider of Client Care

Chapter 4:   Resource Management, Safe Use of Equipment, and Handling Infectious and Hazardous Materials
Contributors: Mary Sue Marz, PhD, RN
                 Karin K. Roberts, PhD, RN

 NCLEX® Connections:

Learning Objective: Review and apply knowledge within "**Resource Management, Safe Use of Equipment, and Handling Infectious and Hazardous Materials**" in readiness for performance of the following nursing activities as outlined by the NCLEX® test plans:

Δ   Plan for and use cost-effective measures when providing client care.

Δ   Continuously assess clients' needs for materials and equipment.

Δ   Continuously assess staff's use of cost-effective measures and intervene to maintain cost-effectiveness.

Δ   Assess the client and staff's correct use of materials and equipment, teach proper use, and intervene to ensure effective use as needed.

Δ   Intervene to control the spread of infectious agents per agency policies.

Δ   Continuously assess the environment for biohazardous, flammable, and infectious materials and follow procedures to maintain client/staff safety.

Δ   Report work environment conditions that pose a risk to client/staff safety.

Δ   Promote safe use of equipment per agency procedures (e.g., routinely check equipment for safe functioning, promptly remove and report any malfunctioning equipment).

 Key Points

Δ   **Resource Management**

•   Resources (e.g., supplies, equipment, personnel) are critical to accomplishing the goals and objectives in a health care facility.

•   Resource management includes **budgeting** and **resource allocation**.

◊   Budgeting is usually the responsibility of the unit manager, but the staff nurse may be asked to provide input.

◊   Resource allocation is a responsibility of the unit manager as well as every practicing nurse. Providing cost-effective client care should be balanced with quality of care.

Δ   **Safe Use of Equipment**

- Environmental safety within a health care facility influences clients and employees.

Influence on Clients	Influence on Employees
• Reduces incidence of illness and injury. • Prevents extension of the length of treatment and hospitalization. • Improves or preserves a client's functional status. • Increases the client's sense of well-being.	• Allows work to be performed at optimal level. • Minimizes exposure to communicable pathogens. • Reduces the risk of injury.

- Equipment-related injuries may occur as a result of malfunction, disrepair, mishandling of mechanical equipment, or electrocution.

Δ   **Handling Infectious and Hazardous Materials**

- **Infection Control**

  ◊   Infection control is extremely important to prevent cross-contamination and nosocomial infections.

  ° Clients suspected of, or diagnosed with, a communicable disease should be placed in appropriate isolation.

  ° The nurse should ensure that appropriate equipment is available and that isolation procedures are properly carried out by all health care team members.

  ° Staff education regarding infection prevention and control is a responsibility of the nurse.

  ° Facility policies and procedures should serve as a resource for proper implementation of infection prevention and control.

  ◊   Use of standard precautions by all members of the health care team should be enforced. Employees who are allergic to latex should have nonlatex gloves made available to them.

  ◊   Handwashing facilities must be readily accessible to employees in client care areas.

  ◊   Sturdy, moisture-resistant bags should be used for soiled items, and the bags should be tied securely with a knot at the top.

  ◊   Sharps containers should be readily available in client care areas, and any needlestick involving an employee should be reported in accordance with facility policy and state law.

- **Hazardous Materials**

  ◊ Nurses and other members of the health care team are at risk for exposure to hazardous materials.

  ◊ Employees have the right to refuse to work in hazardous working conditions if there is a clear threat to their health.

  ◊ Health care team members should follow occupational safety and health guidelines as set by the Occupational Safety and Health Administration (OSHA). Guidelines include:

    ° Providing each employee a place of employment that is free from recognized hazards that can cause or are likely to cause death or serious physical harm.

    ° Making protective gear accessible to employees working under hazardous conditions or with hazardous materials (e.g., antineoplastic medications, sterilization chemicals).

    ° Providing measurement devices and keeping records that document an employee's level of exposure over time to hazardous materials, such as radiation from x-rays.

    ° Providing education and recertification opportunities to each employee regarding these rules and regulations, such as handling of hazardous materials.

    ° Maintaining a manual available to all employees, usually in a central location, that outlines proper procedures for containment of hazardous materials.

    ° Designating an institutional hazardous materials response (HAZMAT) team that responds to handle and control leaks or spills.

Nursing Interventions

Δ **Resource Management**

- **Cost-effective** resource allocation includes:

  ◊ Providing necessary equipment and properly charging the client.

  ◊ Returning uncontaminated, unused equipment to the appropriate department for credit.

  ◊ Using equipment properly to prevent wastage.

  ◊ Providing training to staff unfamiliar with equipment.

  ◊ Returning equipment (e.g., IV, kangaroo pumps) to the proper department (e.g., central service, central distribution) as soon as it is no longer needed. This action will prevent further cost to the client.

Δ **Safe Use of Equipment**

- Strategies to prevent equipment-related injuries include:

   ◊ Maintaining competency in use of equipment.

   ◊ Learning how to properly operate new equipment.

   ◊ Checking that equipment is accurately set and functioning properly (e.g., oxygen, nasogastric suction).

   ◊ Equipping all electrical equipment with a three-prong ground plug.

   ◊ Ensuring that life-support equipment is plugged into outlets designated to be powered by a backup generator during power outages.

   ◊ Removing nonworking equipment from the client care area and sending it to the proper department for repair or disposal.

Δ **Handling Infectious and Hazardous Materials**

- Clean and maintain equipment that is shared by several clients on a unit (e.g., blood pressure cuffs, thermometers, pulse oximeters).

- Use standard precautions at all times.

- Employ proper handwashing techniques.

- Use needlestick precautions when administering parenteral medications.

- Maintain knowledge of rules and regulations and proper procedures for handling infectious/hazardous materials (e.g., use of red biohazard bag for disposal of contaminated materials, proper use of puncture-proof containers for needles).

Primary Reference:

Marquis, B. L., & Huston, C. J. (2006). *Leadership roles and management functions in nursing: Theory and application* (5th ed.). Philadelphia: Lippincott Williams & Wilkins.

Additional Resources:

Hood, L. J., & Leddy, S. K. (2006). *Leddy & Pepper's conceptual bases of professional nursing* (6th ed.). Philadelphia: Lippincott Williams & Wilkins.

Potter, P. A., & Perry, A. G. (2005). *Fundamentals of nursing* (6th ed.). St. Louis, MO: Mosby.

For information about the Occupational Safety and Health Administration, go to the OSHA Web site, *www.osha.gov.*

Chapter 4: Resource Management, Safe Use of Equipment, and Handling Infectious and Hazardous Materials

Application Exercises

1. A nurse observes an assistive personnel (AP) discarding an unused package of gauze pads into the trash. The pads were to be used for a client who requires frequent dressing changes on a decubitus ulcer. Which of the following actions should the nurse take? (Select all that apply.)

   _____ Remove the package of gauze pads from the trash and place it in a box of dressing change equipment.

   _____ Explain to the AP that if the packages are not opened they should be left on the table or placed in the box of dressing change equipment.

   _____ Leave the gauze package in the trash but check that there is a proper place in the room to store unused equipment.

   _____ Remove all unused equipment from the client's room and return it to the equipment store room.

2. A nurse is assigned to a unit on which she does not usually work. When arriving on the unit, she explains that she is allergic to latex and must have nonlatex gloves. The charge nurse explains that they ran out yesterday and none are currently available. Which of the following actions should the nurse take next?

   A. Ask the charge nurse to order a box of gloves for her from the central distribution center.

   B. Not wear gloves and use good handwashing when indicated.

   C. Return to her original unit and borrow a box of nonlatex gloves.

   D. Fill out a grievance form and refuse to provide client care on the unit.

3. A nurse is taking report at the start of his shift. The Kardex indicates that the client in room 202 has an IV attached to an infusion pump running at 125 mL/hr, a nasogastric (NG) tube on intermittent suction at 60 mm Hg, oxygen at 2 L/min per nasal canula, and a sequential compression device providing intermittent compression to the lower extremities. What should the nurse assess to ensure safe use of the client's equipment?

4. The agency that develops regulations to protect employees from working in a hazardous environment is the _____.

5. Describe measures that are taken to ensure that blood glucose monitoring machines are accurately recording a client's blood glucose level.

Chapter 4: Resource Management, Safe Use of Equipment, and Handling Infectious and Hazardous Materials

Application Exercises Answer Key

1. A nurse observes an assistive personnel (AP) discarding an unused package of gauze pads into the trash. The pads were to be used for a client who requires frequent dressing changes on a decubitus ulcer. Which of the following actions should the nurse take? (Select all that apply.)

_____ Remove the package of gauze pads from the trash and place it in a box of dressing change equipment.

X **Explain to the AP that if the packages are not opened they should be left on the table or placed in the box of dressing change equipment.**

X **Leave the gauze package in the trash but check that there is a proper place in the room to store unused equipment.**

_____ Remove all unused equipment from the client's room and return it to the equipment store room.

The nurse should instruct the AP on proper disposition of unopened and unused equipment. It is acceptable to keep a supply of anticipated equipment in the room to reduce time spent searching the equipment room. However, these materials should be kept in a box or other container and not left in random places throughout the room. Even though the package of gauze pads was unopened, it should not be removed from the trash can due to possible cross-contamination from other refuse in the trash can.

2. A nurse is assigned to a unit on which she does not usually work. When arriving on the unit, she explains that she is allergic to latex and must have nonlatex gloves. The charge nurse explains that they ran out yesterday and none are currently available. Which of the following actions should the nurse take next?

    A. Ask the charge nurse to order a box of gloves for her from the central distribution center.

    B. Not wear gloves and use good handwashing when indicated.

    C. Return to her original unit and borrow a box of nonlatex gloves.

    D. Fill out a grievance form and refuse to provide client care on the unit.

It is the responsibility of a health care facility to provide necessary safety equipment for the protection of employees from hazardous materials, including potentially infectious body fluids. Subsequently, the nurse should ask the charge nurse to order a box of gloves immediately for her use and not to start care until the gloves are available. Good handwashing technique can be effective in preventing cross-contamination, but it does not protect the nurse from microbes. It would not be appropriate to borrow a box of gloves from her original unit since the charge for the gloves should come from the other unit's budget. Filing a grievance should not be done unless the proper equipment is not provided in a timely manner.

3. A nurse is taking report at the start of his shift. The Kardex indicates that the client in room 202 has an IV attached to an infusion pump running at 125 mL/hr, a nasogastric (NG) tube on intermittent suction at 60 mm Hg, oxygen at 2 L/min per nasal canula, and a sequential compression device providing intermittent compression to the lower extremities. What should the nurse assess to ensure safe use of the client's equipment?

The nurse's assessment should include checking that: the infusion pump is set at the correct rate (125 mL/hr), the correct fluid is infusing, the line is free of kinks, and the insertion site is warm, pink and dry; the NG suction is set at 60 mm Hg, the NG tube is patent, the amount and appearance of the drainage is normal, and the tube is secured to the client's gown; the nasal canula is properly placed on the client and the oxygen flow meter is set at 2 L/min; the sequential compression device is set at the appropriate pressure and is functioning properly, the stockings are properly placed, and the client's lower extremities are warm with pink skin, palpable pedal pulses, brisk capillary refill, and intact sensation.

4. The agency that develops regulations to protect employees from working in a hazardous environment is the _____.

Occupational Safety and Health Administration

5. Describe measures that are taken to ensure that blood glucose monitoring machines are accurately recording a client's blood glucose level.

Health care team members who use blood glucose monitoring machines are expected to maintain competency in operation of the equipment. This may be done by recertification or completion of competency exercises. It is the responsibility of the nurse to ensure that the test strips have not expired and that the monitor has been calibrated for those specific test strips. Machines will be checked for accuracy and proper functioning on a regular basis per facility policy.

Unit 2   Provider of Client Care

Chapter 5:   **Injury Prevention, Security Plans, and Reporting Incidents**

Contributors: Karin K. Roberts, PhD, RN

Polly Gerber Zimmermann, MS, MBA, RN, CEN, FAEN

 NCLEX® Connections:

Learning Objective: Review and apply knowledge within **"Injury Prevention, Security Plans, and Reporting Incidents"** in readiness for performance of the following nursing activities as outlined by the NCLEX® test plans:

Δ   Recognize client and environmental factors that contribute to accidents and take preventive measures as appropriate.

Δ   Intervene to provide for the client's safety (e.g., check client allergies, take medication error precautions, report environmental hazards, use bed alarms, utilize medical alert bracelets).

Δ   Evaluate outcomes of preventive actions and revise procedures as appropriate.

Δ   Follow the facility's security plan.

Δ   Recognize situations requiring completion of incident/variance reports.

Δ   Report incidents/variances per facility policy.

 Key Points

Δ   **Accidents and Injuries in the Health Care Environment**

- Infants, children, and older adult clients are at an increased risk for accidents and injuries due to their cognitive and physical developmental stage.

- Risks in the health care environment

  ◊   **Falls**

    ° Falls are responsible for 90% of client-related accidents reported in health care institutions.

    ° Older adult clients and clients who are frail have a significantly higher rate of falls.

    ° Risk factors include a history of falls, balance and mobility problems, postural hypotension, sensory impairment, and medication side effects/interactions.

- A major precipitating factor is the client attempting to get out of bed to go to the toilet.

- Clients who experience a fall may have a longer stay in the health care facility, increasing their risk for additional complications.

◊ **Procedure-related accidents**

- Medication and fluid administration errors (e.g., anaphylaxis, fluid overload, fluid deficit)

- Improper application of therapeutic devices, such as improper placement of a continuous passive motion therapy machine (can cause injury if used after knee joint replacement surgery)

- Improper performance of procedures, such as violating sterile technique during catheter insertion (can lead to infection)

◊ **Equipment-related accidents** (*Refer to chapter 4, Resource Management, Safe Use of Equipment, and Handling Infectious and Hazardous Materials.*)

Δ **Security Plans**

- Security issues faced by health care facilities include: admission of potentially dangerous individuals, vandalism, infant abduction, and information theft.

- All health care facilities should have a security management plan in place.

- Recommendations from the International Association for Healthcare Security & Safety (IAHSS) include development of a plan that has preventive, protective, and response measures designed for identified security needs.

- Security measures include:

  ◊ An identification system that identifies employees, volunteers, physicians, students, and regularly scheduled contract services staff as authorized personnel of the health care facility.

  ◊ Electronic security systems in high-risk areas (e.g., the newborn nursery to prevent infant abductions, the emergency department to prevent unauthorized entrants). Examples include:

    - Key code access into and out of newborn nurseries.

    - Wrist bands that electronically link the mother and her infant.

    - Alarms integrated with closed-circuit television cameras. Alarm activation may automatically integrate with monitoring cameras with a view of the alarm location.

- Various code designations for emergencies include:

  ◊ Code Red (fire).

  ◊ Code Pink (newborn abduction).

  ◊ Code Orange (chemical spill).

  ◊ Code Blue (mass casualty incident).

Δ Incident Reports

- Incident reports are records made of unexpected or unusual incidents that occurred when a client was in a health care facility. Incident reports include:

    ◊ Medication errors.

    ◊ Client falls.

    ◊ Accidental omission of a therapy.

    ◊ Needlestick injury.

- Incident reports:

    ◊ Are considered confidential and are not shared with the client.

    ◊ Include a description of the incident and actions taken to safeguard the client and/or assessment and treatment for injuries sustained.

    ◊ Are not placed in the client's chart but are usually handled by a risk management department or officer (varies from facility to facility).

Nursing Interventions

Δ Identify the client at risk and monitor for accidents.

- Use standardized assessment tools to assess for a fall risk (e.g., Morse Fall Scale, the STRATIFY tool, the Hendrich II Fall Risk Model, or the Schmid Fall Risk Assessment Tool) at time of admission and as indicated.

Δ Follow the six rights of medication administration (right medication, dose, client, route, time, and documentation) and maintain up-to-date knowledge base.

Δ Clearly mark the charts of clients with allergies and apply wrist bands identifying the allergies.

Δ Place beds in the low position, use bed and wheelchair alarms, and keep personal items within reach (e.g., phone, nurse call light).

Δ Closely monitor the client with a history of seizures and implement seizure precautions (padded side rails, no hard or sharp objects in close proximity to the client).

Δ Call for assistance when moving clients and use lifting devices appropriately.

Δ Use a transfer or gait belt when ambulating clients.

Δ Evaluate accidents to identify contributing factors and preventative measures.

Δ Avoid documenting the completion and disposition of an incident report in the client's chart.

Δ Be familiar with procedures and polices that outline proper measures to take when accidents, injuries, or breaches in security occur.

Primary Reference:

Marquis, B. L., & Huston, C. J. (2006). *Leadership roles and management functions in nursing: Theory and application* (5th ed.). Philadelphia: Lippincott Williams & Wilkins.

Additional Resources:

For information about the International Association for Healthcare Security & Safety, go to the IAHSS Web site, *www.iahss.org.*

Chapter 5: Injury Prevention, Security Plans, and Reporting Incidents

Application Exercises

1. Which of the following factors increase a client's risk for falls? (Select all that apply.)

    _____ History of a previous fall

    _____ Reduced vision

    _____ Impaired memory

    _____ Antibiotic therapy

    _____ House slippers

    _____ Kyphosis (hump back curvature of the spine)

2. List the six rights of medication administration and at least three additional things a nurse can do to ensure safe and accurate medication administration.

3. A nurse realizes that he gave a client the antihypertensive medication intended for another client. Number the following actions in the appropriate order in which the nurse should take them.

    _____ Call the client's primary care provider.

    _____ Take the client's vital signs.

    _____ Notify the risk management officer.

    _____ Complete an incident report.

    _____ Instruct the client to remain in bed until further notice.

4. Which of the following are true of incident reports? (Select all that apply.)

    _____ Incidents should be documented in the nursing notes.

    _____ Incident reports are confidential and not shared with the client.

    _____ They include a description of the incident and actions taken.

    _____ A copy of the incident report should be placed in the client's chart.

    _____ A risk management department investigates the incident.

5. A nurse notes that two health care team members who smoke often leave the door to the fire escape unlocked while they go out to smoke a cigarette. Why is this a concern and what should the nurse do?

6. An individual approaches the door of the newborn nursery and knocks on the door for entrance. He explains on the intercom that he is the father of an infant. He is unable to provide the infant's code that was provided to the infant's family. Which of the following actions should the nurse take first?

      A. Ask the man several discriminating questions, such as the mother's name and time of birth, and admit him if he can answer them.

      B. Call security to remove the man from the area.

      C. Ask the man to obtain the infant's code from the mother and then return.

      D. Call a Code Pink as the man could be attempting to abduct the infant.

7. While a charge nurse is at lunch, a nurse covering her responsibilities hears a Code Pink. She is not familiar with this designation and does not know what to do. Who has the primary responsibility for ensuring that the nurse is familiar with security protocol?

      A. Unit manager

      B. Staff development educator

      C. Charge nurse

      D. Nurse covering for charge nurse

Chapter 5: Injury Prevention, Security Plans, and Reporting Incidents

Application Exercises Answer Key

1. Which of the following factors increase a client's risk for falls? (Select all that apply.)

   X **History of a previous fall**
   X **Reduced vision**
   X **Impaired memory**
   _____ Antibiotic therapy
   X **House slippers**
   X **Kyphosis (hump back curvature of the spine)**

All of the above factors except antibiotic therapy can increase a client's risk for falls. A history of falls is a significant risk factor; reduced vision may make it difficult for the client to avoid mishaps with equipment and furniture in the environment; clients with impaired memory may find it difficult to remember instructions such as using the call light to ask for help to get to the toilet; house slippers may not provide adequate traction and support for safe ambulation; and kyphosis alters an individual's posture and center of balance.

2. List the six rights of medication administration and at least three additional things a nurse can do to ensure safe and accurate medication administration.

Right medication, dose, client, route, time, and documentation

The nurse should also focus solely on preparing medication without other distractions at that time, should never administer a medication prepared by another nurse, and should know the mechanism of action, side effects, and nursing implications of all medications administered.

3. A nurse realizes that he gave a client the antihypertensive medication intended for another client. Number the following actions in the appropriate order in which the nurse should take them.

   3   Call the client's primary care provider.

   1   Take the client's vital signs.

   5   Notify the risk management officer.

   4   Complete an incident report.

   2   Instruct the client to remain in bed until further notice.

Since the medication administered can decrease blood pressure, the nurse should take the client's vital signs and instruct the client to remain in bed until the medication's effects can be assessed. The primary care provider should then be notified of the error. He then may order a medication to counteract the medication's effects if the client's vital signs indicate this is necessary. The nurse must then complete an incident report and notify the risk management officer for proper disposition.

4. Which of the following are true of incident reports? (Select all that apply.)

   _____   Incidents should be documented in the nursing notes.

   X   **Incident reports are confidential and not shared with the client.**

   X   **They include a description of the incident and actions taken.**

   _____   A copy of the incident report should be placed in the client's chart.

   X   **A risk management department investigates the incident.**

An incident report is confidential and not shared with the client. An incident report should include a description of the incident and actions taken to safeguard the client and/or assess and treat injuries sustained. A risk management department usually investigates the incident. A copy of the incident report should not be placed in the client's chart, nor should it be documented in the nursing notes that a report was completed.

5. A nurse notes that two health care team members who smoke often leave the door to the fire escape unlocked while they go out to smoke a cigarette. Why is this a concern and what should the nurse do?

This is a concern for several reasons. First, a safety issue exists in relation to providing an unsafe exit for clients who may be confused and disoriented. Second, if the exit is left unlocked, unauthorized individuals could enter the institution. The nurse should explain that this is against hospital policy and ask that the team members smoke in a designated area and leave the fire exit locked. If they do not comply, the appropriate unit manager or supervisor should be notified for appropriate disciplinary action.

6. An individual approaches the door of the newborn nursery and knocks on the door for entrance. He explains on the intercom that he is the father of an infant. He is unable to provide the infant's code that was provided to the infant's family. Which of the following actions should the nurse take first?

    A. Ask the man several discriminating questions, such as the mother's name and time of birth, and admit him if he can answer them.

    B. Call security to remove the man from the area.

    C. Ask the man to obtain the infant's code from the mother and then return.

    D. Call a Code Pink as the man could be attempting to abduct the infant.

The nurse should initially ask the man to obtain the proper code from the infant's mother. If he returns with the code, he should be admitted. While asking the man discriminating questions may verify that he is the father, it does not follow the safety procedures outlined by the facility. It is premature to involve security or call a Code Pink, since the man has not made any threatening gestures that would warrant these actions.

7. While a charge nurse is at lunch, a nurse covering her responsibilities hears a Code Pink. She is not familiar with this designation and does not know what to do. Who has the primary responsibility for ensuring that the nurse is familiar with security protocol?

    A. Unit manager

    B. Staff development educator

    C. Charge nurse

    D. Nurse covering for charge nurse

While all of the above individuals have some responsibility to ensure that health team members responsible for client care are knowledgeable about safety and security protocols, all health care team members, including the nurse who is covering for the charge nurse, should be familiar with these highly important protocols.

Unit 2   Provider of Client Care

Chapter 6:   Prioritizing Client Care

Contributors: Jeanne Wissmann, PhD, RN, CNE
Polly Gerber Zimmermann, MS, MBA, RN, CEN, FAEN

 NCLEX® Connections:

Learning Objective: Review and apply knowledge within "**Prioritizing Client Care**" in readiness for performance of the following nursing activities as outlined by the NCLEX® test plans:

Δ   Prioritize the order of care delivery for a caseload of clients based on the clients' current condition.

Δ   Prioritize and plan care for a caseload of clients based on verbal and written reports and documentation.

Δ   Prioritize client care based on assessment of assigned clients' current conditions.

Δ   Recognize changes in the client's status and promptly notify other members of the health care team.

Δ   Evaluate client outcome achievement and revise plan of care as needed.

 Key Points

Δ   Nurses must continuously set and reset **priorities** in order to meet the needs of multiple clients and to maintain client safety.

Δ   **Priority setting** involves decision making regarding the order in which:

•   Clients are seen.

•   Assessments are completed.

•   Interventions are provided.

•   Steps in a client procedure are completed.

•   Components of client care are completed.

Δ   Prioritization involves **organizing** activities from **most important** to **least important**.

Δ   Establishing priorities in nursing practice requires **decision making** (urgent/ routine) based on **evidence**. Clinical evidence important to priority setting is gathered:

- During shift reports and other communications among the health care team.

- Through careful review of documents.

- By continuously and accurately assessing clients.

Prioritization Principles in Client Care	
Principle	**Examples**
Systemic before local ("life before limb")	• Prioritizing interventions for a client in shock over interventions for a client with a localized limb injury
Acute (less opportunity for physical adaptation) before chronic (greater opportunity for physical adaptation)	• Prioritizing care of a client with a new injury/ illness (e.g., mental confusion, chest pain) or experiencing an acute exacerbation over care of a client with a long-term chronic illness
Actual problems before potential future problems	• Prioritizing administration of medication to a client experiencing acute pain over ambulation of a client at risk for thrombophlebitis
Listen carefully to clients and don't assume.	• Responding to a client's report that the pain is the same as the pain he experienced with his last heart attack • Recognizing that a client's report of postoperative pain could be due to something other than expected surgical pain
Recognize and respond to trends.	• Recognizing a gradual deterioration in a client's level of consciousness
Recognize signs of medical emergencies and complications versus "expected client findings."	• Recognizing signs of increasing intracranial pressure versus the clinical findings expected following a stroke
Apply clinical knowledge to priority setting.	• Recognizing that the timing of administration of antidiabetic and antimicrobial medications is more important than administration of a routine daily medication • Recognizing the potential risks associated with specific health alterations, such as immunosuppression due to cancer treatment

Priority Setting Frameworks

Δ   Maslow's Hierarchy

- The nurse should consider this hierarchy of human needs when prioritizing interventions. For example, the nurse should prioritize the client's:

  ◊   Need for airway and oxygen over a need for sleep.

  ◊   Physiological need for pain relief over the client's safety need for employment.

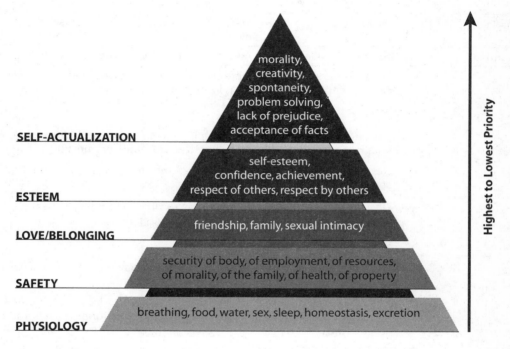

Adapted from: *http://commons.wikimedia.org/wiki/Image:Maslow%27s_hierarchy_of_needs.png*
Copyright © 2007 Assessment Technologies Institute®.
Permission is granted to copy, distribute, and/or modify this document under the terms of the GNU Free Documentation License, Version 1.2 or any later version published by the Free Software Foundation; with no Invariant Sections, no Front-Cover texts, and no Back-Cover texts. A copy of the license is included in the section entitled "GNU Free Documentation License."

△   **Airway Breathing Circulation Disability (ABCD)**

Priority	Assessment	Interventions
First	Airway	• Identify an airway concern (e.g., apnea, stridor, intermittent breathing pattern). • Establish patent airway if indicated. • Recognize that every moment without a patent airway poses a risk for cerebral anoxia.
Second	Breathing	• Assess the effectiveness of the client's breathing. • Intervene as needed.
Third	Circulation	• Identify circulation needs (e.g., hypotension, dysrhythmia, inadequate cardiac output).
Fourth	Disability	• Assess for disability, such as neurological deficits.

• Consider the severity of symptoms when determining priorities. A severe circulation problem may take priority over a minor breathing problem.

△   **Safety/Risk Reduction**

• Look first for a safety risk. For example, is there a finding that suggests a risk for airway obstruction, hypoxia, bleeding, infection, or injury?

• Next ask, "What's the risk to the client?" and "How significant is the risk compared to other posed risks?"

• Give priority to intervening/responding to whatever finding poses the greatest (or most imminent) risk to the client's physical well-being.

△   **Assessment First**

• Use the nursing process to gather pertinent information prior to making a nursing diagnosis or creating a plan of intervention.

◊   For example, determine if additional assessment information is needed prior to calling the primary care provider to ask for pain medication for a client.

△   **Survival Potential**

• Use this framework in situations in which health resources are extremely limited (e.g., disaster triage).

• Give priority to clients who have a reasonable chance of survival with prompt intervention. Clients who have a limited likelihood of survival even with intense intervention are assigned the lowest priority.

Δ   **Least Restrictive**

- Select interventions that maintain client safety while posing the least amount of restriction to the client.

- For example, if a client with a high fall risk index is getting out of bed without assistance, move the client closer to the nurses' work area rather than choosing to apply restraints.

Primary Reference:

Marquis, B. L., & Huston, C. J. (2006). *Leadership roles and management functions in nursing: Theory and application* (5th ed.). Philadelphia: Lippincott Williams & Wilkins.

Additional Resources:

Zimmermann, P. G. (2002, February). Guiding principles at triage: Advice for new triage nurses. *Journal of Emergency Nursing, 28*(1), 24-33.

Chapter 6: Prioritizing Client Care

Application Exercises

1. A nurse receives a change-of-shift report at 0700 for an assigned caseload of clients. Number the following clients in the order in which they should be seen.

_____ A client who has been receiving a blood transfusion since 0400

_____ A client who has an every 4 hr PRN analgesic order and who last received pain medication at 0430

_____ A client who is going for a colonoscopy at 1130 and whose informed consent needs to be verified

_____ A client who needs rapid onset insulin when the 0800 trays arrive

_____ A client who is being discharged today and needs reinforcement of teaching regarding dressing changes

2. An older adult client who is on fall precautions is found lying on the floor of his hospital room. Which of the following actions is most appropriate for the nurse to take first?

   A. Call the client's primary care provider.

   B. Carefully move the client to his bed.

   C. Palpate the client's wrist and evaluate his pulse.

   D. Ask the client why he got out of bed without assistance.

3. A nurse is assigned to care for four clients. Number the following clients in the order in which they should be seen.

_____ 38-year-old female client with a history of gallstones admitted with right upper quadrant pain that radiates to the right shoulder. No report of pain for the past several hours.

_____ 59-year-old male admitted with acute pancreatitis. He is reporting a pain level of 8/10 despite medication. He has a glucose level of 225 g/dL and a WBC count of 19,500/mm^3.

_____ 60-year-old female client receiving IV antimicrobials every 6 hr via a central line. She has an NG tube in place that is to be removed later today.

_____ 30-year-old male who appears frail and malnourished. He has been experiencing severe diarrhea. He is receiving total parenteral nutrition (TPN) through a central line.

Scenario: A nurse receives the following change-of-shift report:

> 28-year-old female admitted yesterday
> Diagnosis: Peritonitis secondary to a ruptured appendix
> Vital signs: T101° F – P108/min – R26/min – BP148/78 mm Hg
> Oxygen 1 L/min per nasal cannula
> Pulse oximetry readings have decreased from 99% to 89% over the last 4 hr
> NPO except for ice chips
> JP drain: brown purulent fluid moderate amount
> $D_5\frac{1}{2}NS$ @ 100 mL/hr via subclavian IV
> Morphine PCA, gentamicin (Gentacidin), ceftriaxone (Rocephin)
> AM Lab Results:
> > Hemoglobin 12.0 g/dL (preop 12.8 g/dL)
> > Hematocrit 37% (preop 39%)
> > Platelets 165,000/mm³ (preop 150,000/mm³)
> > White blood cells 23,500/mm³ (preop 18,700/mm³)

4. Based on the information provided in the change-of-shift report, the nurse should assign initial priority to which of the following reported client findings?

    A. JP drainage

    B. Tachycardia

    C. Elevated temperature

    D. Oxygen saturation level

5. Which laboratory finding should be assigned the highest priority?

6. Based on the change-of-shift report, what are appropriate priorities for this client's plan of care?

Chapter 6: Prioritizing Client Care

Application Exercises Answer Key

1. A nurse receives a change-of-shift report at 0700 for an assigned caseload of clients. Number the following clients in the order in which they should be seen.

   1   A client who has been receiving a blood transfusion since 0400

   3   A client who has an every 4 hr PRN analgesic order and who last received pain medication at 0430

   4   A client who is going for a colonoscopy at 1130 and whose informed consent needs to be verified

   2   A client who needs rapid onset insulin when the 0800 trays arrive

   5   A client who is being discharged today and needs reinforcement of teaching regarding dressing changes

   1. The blood transfusion should not extend beyond 4 hr of infusion time. The nurse needs to check to make sure the client is tolerating the infusion well and that the transfusion is infusing correctly and is on time.
   2. The insulin will need to be administered at 0800.
   3. The nurse will need to evaluate for administration of an analgesic around 0830.
   4. The nurse should then verify that the informed consent is completed so as to allow sufficient time in case the nurse needs to take any action prior to the scheduled colonoscopy.
   5. The discharge teaching needs to be completed prior to discharge but is not as time sensitive as the other client interventions.

2. An older adult client who is on fall precautions is found lying on the floor of his hospital room. Which of the following actions is most appropriate for the nurse to take first?

   A. Call the client's primary care provider.

   B. Carefully move the client to his bed.

   C. Palpate the client's wrist and evaluate his pulse.

   D. Ask the client why he got out of bed without assistance.

   It is most important to establish systemic stability. The nurse needs to determine if emergency interventions are indicated. If emergency interventions are not indicated, the nurse should perform a focused assessment prior to calling the primary care provider. The client should not be moved without first determining the need for neck immobilization. Assessing the client's current condition is a priority rather than understanding the reason that the client attempted ambulation without assistance.

3. A nurse is assigned to care for four clients. Number the following clients in the order in which they should be seen.

___4___ 38-year-old female client with a history of gallstones admitted with right upper quadrant pain that radiates to the right shoulder. No report of pain for the past several hours.

___1___ 59-year-old male admitted with acute pancreatitis. He is reporting a pain level of 8/10 despite medication. He has a glucose level of 225 g/dL and a WBC count of 19,500/mm³.

___3___ 60-year-old female client receiving IV antimicrobials every 6 hr via a central line. She has an NG tube in place that is to be removed later today.

___2___ 30-year-old male who appears frail and malnourished. He has been experiencing severe diarrhea. He is receiving total parenteral nutrition (TPN) through a central line.

1. The client with acute pancreatitis is in severe pain, and his laboratory values are of concern.
2. The client experiencing repeated bouts of diarrhea is at considerable risk for serious fluid and electrolyte imbalances, and TPN therapy requires close monitoring.
3. The client receiving antimicrobial therapy via a central line should be assessed next.
4. The client with possible cholecystitis should be assessed, although based on initial reports the client's pain has resolved.

Scenario: A nurse receives the following change-of-shift report:

> 28-year-old female admitted yesterday
> Diagnosis: Peritonitis secondary to a ruptured appendix
> Vital signs: T101° F – P108/min – R26/min – BP148/78 mm Hg
> Oxygen 1 L/min per nasal cannula
> Pulse oximetry readings have decreased from 99% to 89% over the last 4 hr
> NPO except for ice chips
> JP drain: brown purulent fluid moderate amount
> $D_5\frac{1}{2}NS$ @ 100 mL/hr via subclavian IV
> Morphine PCA, gentamicin (Gentacidin), ceftriaxone (Rocephin)
> AM Lab Results:
>> Hemoglobin 12.0 g/dL (preop 12.8 g/dL)
>> Hematocrit 37% (preop 39%)
>> Platelets 165,000/mm³ (preop 150,000/mm³)
>> White blood cells 23,500/mm³ (preop 18,700/mm³)

4. Based on the information provided in the change-of-shift report, the nurse should assign initial priority to which of the following reported client findings?

        A. JP drainage

        B. Tachycardia

        C. Elevated temperature

        D. Oxygen saturation level

The change in the client's respiratory status is the client finding with the highest priority. The other findings will need further investigation as well but are not more important than the client's breathing status.

5. Which laboratory finding should be assigned the highest priority?

The increased WBC count is an indicator of infection. An increase in WBC count after 24 hr of antimicrobial therapy may indicate that a different antimicrobial is needed. The other laboratory values are normal findings following surgery.

6. Based on the change-of-shift report, what are appropriate priorities for this client's plan of care?

Evaluation of respiratory distress – potential for acute respiratory failure
Evaluation of infection – evidence supports serious infection without evidence of resolution (fever, elevated WBC)
Evaluation of the client's fluid and electrolyte balance – no electrolytes in IV, slight decrease in hematocrit and hemoglobin (blood loss)
Pain management – monitoring for complications and evidence of effectiveness
Wound management – monitoring JP and wound drainage, assessing incision site
Antimicrobial therapy – administration and monitoring for complications and evidence of effectiveness

Unit 3   Supervisor of Client Care

Chapter 7:	Assigning, Delegating, and Supervising Client Care

Contributors: Angela M. Balistrieri, MSN, RN
             Annette C. Milius, MA, RN, APRN-BC

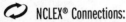 **NCLEX® Connections:**

Learning Objective: Review and apply knowledge within "**Assigning, Delegating, and Supervising Client Care**" in readiness for performance of the following nursing activities as outlined by the NCLEX® test plans:

Δ   Assess client needs and assign clients to appropriate staff based on level of care needed.

Δ   Make appropriate client room assignments based on level of care needed.

Δ   Identify tasks that can be delegated to other members of the health care team.

Δ   Assess and ensure ability (e.g., knowledge, skill level, experience) of health care team members when delegating responsibilities.

Δ   Provide accurate, concise reports to assist health care team members in their performance of delegated tasks, and instruct when to seek assistance immediately.

Δ   Delegate appropriate tasks to assistive personnel using the five rights of delegation.

Δ   Provide supervision to health care team members who are performing delegated tasks.

Δ   Perform ongoing monitoring of interventions performed by other members of the health care team and intervene as needed.

Δ   Evaluate and document delegated care.

 Key Points

Δ   **Assignment** is the process of transferring both the responsibility and accountability of client care to another member of the health care team.

Δ   **Delegation** is transferring the authority and responsibility to another to complete a task, while maintaining the **accountability**.

Δ   The registered nurse (RN) is responsible for providing clear directions when a task is initially delegated and for periodic reassessment and evaluation of the outcome of the task.

Δ **Supervision** is the process of directing, overseeing, and monitoring the performance of tasks by another member of the health care team. RNs have responsibility for supervising client care tasks delegated to assistive personnel (AP) and licensed practical nurses (LPNs) – also known as licensed vocational nurses (LVNs).

Key Factors

Δ **Assignment Factors**

- Client factors

    ◊ Complexity of care needed

    ◊ Specific care needs (e.g., cardiac monitoring, mechanical ventilation)

    ◊ Need for special precautions (e.g., private room with negative air pressure and anteroom, fall precautions, seizure precautions)

- Health care team factors

    ◊ Skills

    ◊ Experience

    ◊ Nurse-to-client ratio

Δ **Delegation Factors**

- **Task factors** – Prior to delegating client care, the nurse should consider:

    ◊ Predictability of outcome.

        ° Will the completion of the task have a predictable outcome?

        ° Is it a routine treatment?

        ° Is it a new treatment?

    ◊ Potential for harm.

        ° Is there a chance that something negative may happen to the client (e.g., risk for bleeding, risk for aspiration)?

        ° Is the client unstable?

    ◊ Complexity of care.

        ° More complex tasks should not be delegated.

    ◊ Need for problem solving and innovation.

        ° Will a judgment need to be made while performing the task?

        ° Does it require nursing assessment skills?

    ◊ Level of interaction with the client.

        ° Is there a need to provide psychosocial support or education during the performance of the task?

- **Delegatee factors** – Considerations for selection of an appropriate delegatee include:

  ◊ Education, training, and experience.

  ◊ Knowledge and skill to perform the task.

  ◊ Level of critical thinking required to complete the task.

  ◊ Ability to communicate with others as it pertains to the duty.

  ◊ Demonstrated competence.

  ◊ Agency policies and procedures.

  ◊ Licensing legislation (state nurse practice acts).

Examples of Tasks that an RN Can Delegate	
(provided agency policy and state practice guidelines permit)	
To LPNs	**To AP**
• Monitoring client findings (as input to the RN's ongoing assessment of the client) • Reinforcement of client teaching from a standard care plan • Tracheostomy care • Suctioning • Checking nasogastric tube patency • Administration of enteral feedings • Insertion of a urinary catheter • Medication administration (excluding intravenous medications in several states)	• Activities of daily living (ADLs) • Bathing • Grooming • Dressing • Toileting • Ambulating • Feeding (without swallowing precautions) • Positioning • Bed making • Specimen collection • Intake and output (I&O) • Vital signs

- **Care that cannot be delegated** according to professional practice standards includes care related to:

  ◊ Nursing process.

  ° Assessment

  ° Diagnosis

  ° Planning

  ° Evaluation

  ◊ Nursing judgment.

Delegation and Supervision Guidelines

Δ   Use the **five rights of delegation** to decide: what tasks should be delegated (right task), under what circumstances (right circumstance), to whom (right person), what information should be communicated (right direction/communication), and how to supervise/evaluate (right supervision/evaluation). Use professional judgment and critical thinking skills when delegating.

- **Right task**

    ◊   Identify what tasks are appropriate to delegate for each specific client.

        °   A right task is repetitive, requires little supervision, and is relatively noninvasive for a certain client.

    ◊   Delegate activities to appropriate levels of team members (e.g., LPN, AP) based on professional standards of practice, legal and facility guidelines, and available resources.

Right task	Wrong task
Delegate AP to assist a client with pneumonia to use a bedpan.	Delegate AP to administer a nebulizer treatment to a client with pneumonia.

- **Right circumstance**

    ◊   Assess the health status and complexity of care required by the client.

    ◊   Match the complexity of care demands to the skill level of the health care team member.

    ◊   Consider the workload of the team member.

Right circumstance	Wrong circumstance
Delegate AP to assist in obtaining vital signs from a stable postoperative client.	Delegate AP to assist in obtaining vital signs from a postoperative client who required naloxone (Narcan) for depressed respirations.

- **Right person**

    ◊   Assess and verify the competency of the health care team member.

        °   The task must be within the team member's scope of practice.

        °   The team member must have the necessary competence/training.

    ◊   Continually review the performance of the team member and determine care competency.

    ◊   Assess team member performance based on standards and, when necessary, take steps to remediate failure to meet standards.

Right person	Wrong person
Delegate an LPN to administer enteral feedings to a client with a head injury.	Delegate an AP to administer enteral feedings to a client with a head injury.

- **Right direction/communication** – Communicate either in writing or orally:

  ◊ Data that need to be collected.

  ◊ Method and timeline for reporting, including when to report concerns/assessment findings.

  ◊ Specific task(s) to be performed; client-specific instructions.

  ◊ Expected results, timelines, and expectations for follow-up communication.

Right direction/communication	Wrong direction/communication
Delegate AP the task of assisting the client in room 312 with a shower, to be completed by 0900.	Delegate AP the task of assisting the client in room 312 with morning hygiene.

- **Right supervision/evaluation** – The delegating nurse must:

  ◊ Provide supervision, either directly or indirectly (e.g., assigning supervision to another licensed nurse).

  ◊ Provide clear directions and understandable expectations of the task(s) to be performed (e.g., timeframes, what to report).

  ◊ Monitor performance.

  ◊ Provide feedback.

  ◊ Intervene if necessary (e.g., unsafe clinical practice).

  ◊ Evaluate the client and determine if client outcomes were met.

  ◊ Evaluate client care tasks and identify needs for performance improvement activities and/or additional resources.

Right supervision	Wrong supervision
An RN delegates to an AP the task of ambulating a client after completing the admission assessment.	An RN delegates an AP to ambulate a client prior to performing an admission assessment.

Primary Reference:

Marquis, B. L., & Huston, C. J. (2006). *Leadership roles and management functions in nursing: Theory and application* (5th ed.). Philadelphia: Lippincott Williams & Wilkins.

Additional Resources:

Yoder-Wise, P. S. (2003). *Leading and managing in nursing* (3rd ed.). St. Louis: Mosby.

Chapter 7: Assigning, Delegating, and Supervising Client Care

Application Exercises

1. Based on national guidelines rather than practice within any specific state, identify which team members can perform each of the following tasks. Identify the rationale for RN-only tasks.

Task	AP	LPN	RN
Developing a teaching plan for a client newly diagnosed with diabetes mellitus			
Assessing a client admitted for surgery			
Collecting vital signs every 30 min for a client who is 1 hr post cardiac catheterization			
Calculating a client's intake and output			
Administering blood to a client			
Monitoring a client's condition during blood transfusions and intravenous administrations			
Providing oral and bathing hygiene to an immobilized client			
Initiating client referrals			
Dressing change of an uncomplicated wound			
Routine nasotracheal suctioning			
Receiving report from surgery nurse regarding a client to be admitted to a unit from the PACU			
Initiating a continuous IV infusion of dopamine with dosage titration based on hemodynamic measurements			
Administering subcutaneous insulin			
Assessing and documenting a client's decubitus ulcer			
Evaluating a client's advance directive status			
Providing written information regarding advance directives			
Initial feeding of a client who had a stroke and is at risk for aspiration			
Assisting a client with toileting			
Developing a plan of care for a client			
Administering an oral medication			
Assisting a client with ambulation			
Administering an IM pain medication			
Checking a client's feeding tube placement and patency			
Turning a client every 2 hr			
Calculating and monitoring TPN flow rate			

2. A client has just returned from the surgical suite following a colon resection. Which of the following tasks is appropriate for a nurse to delegate to an AP?

      A. Asking the client about his pain level every hour

      B. Checking the placement of the nasogastric tube at least once a shift

      C. Looking at the client's dressing and determining the amount of drainage every other hour

      D. Obtaining the client's vital signs every hr x 4 and then every 4 hr x 48 hr

3. Which of the following tasks could be assigned to an AP? (Select all that apply.)

   _____ Assisting a client who is experiencing diarrhea with perineal care

   _____ Vitals signs every 2 hr for a client with pancreatitis

   _____ Transportation of a client to the radiology department

   _____ Cleansing the nares of a client with a nasogastric tube

   _____ Assessing a client for perianal excoriation during perineal care

   _____ Reporting the quality and color of a client's nasogastric drainage

4. Toward the end of a shift, an LPN reports to an RN that a recently hired AP has not totaled clients' I&O for the past 8 hr. Which of the following actions should the RN take?

      A. Confront the AP and instruct him to complete the intake and output measurements.

      B. Delegate this task to the LPN since the AP may not have been educated on this task.

      C. Ask the AP if he needs assistance completing the I&O records.

      D. Notify the nurse manager to include this on the AP's evaluation.

5. Match each delegation principle with the correct delegation.

_____ Wrong direction	A. Delegate an LPN to develop a care plan for a newly admitted client.
_____ Wrong task	B. Delegate an AP to assist a confused client to eat.
_____ Right supervision	C. Delegate an AP to empty a Foley drainage bag.
_____ Right circumstance	D. Delegate an LPN to administer insulin without providing the client's blood glucose level.
_____ Right person	E. Delegate an AP to take vital signs for a postoperative client; review charting after 1 hr.

Chapter 7: Assigning, Delegating, and Supervising Client Care

Application Exercises Answer Key

1. Based on national guidelines rather than practice within any specific state, identify which team members can perform each of the following tasks. Identify the rationale for RN-only tasks.

Task	AP	LPN	RN
Developing a teaching plan for a client newly diagnosed with diabetes mellitus			X
Assessing a client admitted for surgery			X
Collecting vital signs every 30 min for a client who is 1 hr post cardiac catheterization	X	X	X
Calculating a client's intake and output	X	X	X
Administering blood to a client			X
Monitoring a client's condition during blood transfusions and intravenous administrations		X	X
Providing oral and bathing hygiene to an immobilized client	X	X	X
Initiating client referrals			X
Dressing change of an uncomplicated wound		X	X
Routine nasotracheal suctioning		X	X
Receiving report from surgery nurse regarding a client to be admitted to a unit from the PACU			X
Initiating a continuous IV infusion of dopamine with dosage titration based on hemodynamic measurements			X
Administering subcutaneous insulin		X	X
Assessing and documenting a client's decubitus ulcer			X
Evaluating a client's advance directive status			X
Providing written information regarding advance directives		X	X
Initial feeding of a client who had a stroke and is at risk for aspiration			X
Assisting a client with toileting	X	X	X
Developing a plan of care for a client			X
Administering an oral medication		X	X
Assisting a client with ambulation	X	X	X
Administering an IM pain medication		X	X
Checking a client's feeding tube placement and patency		X	X
Turning a client every 2 hr	X	X	X
Calculating and monitoring TPN flow rate			X

Rationale for RN-only tasks:
RNs retain accountability for the nursing process – assessment, diagnosis, planning, and evaluation. All tasks that involve the steps of the nursing process can only be performed by an RN. In general, some input measures can be delegated (e.g., I&O, vital signs, reporting client observations), but not responsibility for the process.
Not all state practice acts allow for LPN performance of parenteral medication administration (e.g., blood administration, TPN).
Actions like titration of dopamine and feeding clients at risk for aspiration require nursing judgment.

2. A client has just returned from the surgical suite following a colon resection. Which of the following tasks is appropriate for a nurse to delegate to an AP?

    A. Asking the client about his pain level every hour

    B. Checking the placement of the nasogastric tube at least once a shift

    C. Looking at the client's dressing and determining the amount of drainage every other hour

    D. Obtaining the client's vital signs every hr x 4 and then every 4 hr x 48 hr

Vital sign measurements are typical AP skills. Pain and wound assessments are RN responsibilities. Checking placement of the NG tube is usually an RN/LPN responsibility.

3. Which of the following tasks could be assigned to an AP? (Select all that apply.)

    __X__ **Assisting a client who is experiencing diarrhea with perineal care**

    __X__ **Vitals signs every 2 hr for a client with pancreatitis**

    __X__ **Transportation of a client to the radiology department**

    __X__ **Cleansing the nares of a client with a nasogastric tube**

    _____ Assessing a client for perianal excoriation during perineal care

    _____ Reporting the quality and color of a client's nasogastric drainage

Assessments, such as assessing for perianal excoriation or the color of nasogastric drainage, are not appropriate for delegation to an AP. Client assessment is the responsibility of RNs.

4. Toward the end of a shift, an LPN reports to an RN that a recently hired AP has not totaled clients' I&O for the past 8 hr. Which of the following actions should the RN take?

      A. Confront the AP and instruct him to complete the intake and output measurements.

      B. Delegate this task to the LPN since the AP may not have been educated on this task.

      C. Ask the AP if he needs assistance completing the I&O records.

      D. Notify the nurse manager to include this on the AP's evaluation.

I&O measurements are routine AP tasks; however, the AP is new and may need some assistance. Making assumptions and negative evaluation without direct evidence should be avoided.

5. Match each delegation principle with the correct delegation.

  D Wrong direction

  A Wrong task

  E Right supervision

  B Right circumstance

  C Right person

A. Delegate an LPN to develop a care plan for a newly admitted client.

B. Delegate an AP to assist a confused client to eat.

C. Delegate an AP to empty a Foley drainage bag.

D. Delegate an LPN to administer insulin without providing the client's blood glucose level.

E. Delegate an AP to take vital signs for a postoperative client; review charting after 1 hr.

Delegating an LPN to develop a care plan for a newly admitted client is the <u>wrong task</u>, because an LPN cannot write a care plan.

Delegating an AP to assist a confused client to eat is the <u>right circumstance</u>, because an AP can assist a client to eat, but not in all circumstances (e.g., a client who has had a stroke and has not been evaluated by a speech therapist).

Delegating an AP to empty a Foley drainage bag is the <u>right person</u>, because the task is within the AP scope of practice.

Delegating an LPN to administer insulin without providing the client's blood glucose level is the <u>wrong direction</u>, because the LPN does not have the necessary information to complete this task.

Delegating an AP to take vital signs and reviewing the results after 1 hr is the <u>right supervision</u>, because this is appropriate supervision for this delegation.

Unit 3   Supervisor of Client Care

Chapter 8:   Conflict Resolution
                  Contributor: Karin K. Roberts, PhD, RN

 NCLEX® Connections:

> **Learning Objective**: Review and apply knowledge within "**Conflict Resolution**" in readiness for performance of the following nursing activities as outlined by the NCLEX® test plans:
>
> Δ   Demonstrate the ability to resolve conflicts that arise in the health care facility (e.g., between staff members, between the client and family).
>
> Δ   Participate in conflict resolution between staff members and clients.
>
> Δ   Follow facility policy when participating in conflict resolution.

 Key Points

Δ   **Conflict**

• Conflict is the result of opposing thoughts, ideas, feelings, perceptions, behaviors, values, opinions, or actions between individuals.

• Conflict is an inevitable part of professional, social, and personal life and can result in constructive or destructive consequences.

Constructive Consequences	Destructive Consequences
• Stimulates growth and open and honest communication. • Increases group cohesion and commitment to common goals. • Facilitates understanding and problem solving. • Motivates group to change. • Stimulates creativity.	• Can produce divisiveness. • May foster rivalry and competition. • Misperceptions, distrust, and frustration can be created. • Group dissatisfaction with the outcome may occur.

- Lack of conflict can create organizational stasis, while too much conflict can be demoralizing, produce anxiety, and contribute to burnout.

- The desired goal in resolving conflict is for both parties to reach a satisfactory resolution. This is called a *win-win* solution.

  ◊ A win-win solution is not always possible. There is the possibility of a solution in which one party wins while the other loses, as well as a *lose-lose* solution in which both parties lose.

Δ **Categories of Conflict**

- Intrapersonal

  ◊ Occurs within the person.

  ◊ May involve internal struggle related to contradictory values or wants.

    ° Example: The nurse wants to move up on the career ladder but is finding that time with her family is subsequently compromised.

- Interpersonal

  ◊ Occurs between two or more people with differing values, goals, and/or beliefs.

  ◊ Interpersonal conflict in the health care setting involves disagreement among nurses, clients, family members, and within a health care team.

  ◊ This is a significant issue in nursing, especially in relation to new graduate nurses, who bring new personalities and perspectives to various health care settings.

  ◊ Interpersonal conflict contributes to burnout and work-related stress.

    ° Example: A new graduate is given a client assignment that is heavier than those of other nurses, and when he asks for help, it is denied.

- Inter-group

  ◊ Occurs between two or more groups of individuals, departments, or organizations.

  ◊ May be caused by a new policy or procedure, a change in leadership, or a change in organizational structure.

    ° Example: There is confusion as to whether it is the responsibility of the nursing unit or dietary department to pass meal trays.

Δ **Organizational Conflict**

- Organizational conflict can disrupt working relationships and create a stressful work environment.

- If conflict exists to the level that productivity and quality of care are compromised, the unit manager must attempt to identify the origin of the conflict and attempt to resolve it.

- Common causes of organizational conflict include:

    ◊ Ineffective communication.

    ◊ Unclear expectations of team members in their various roles.

    ◊ Poorly defined or actualized organizational structure.

    ◊ Conflicts of interest and variance in standards.

    ◊ Incompatibility of individuals.

    ◊ Management or staffing changes.

    ◊ Diversity related to age, gender, race, and ethnicity.

Δ **Negotiation**

- Negotiation is the process by which interested parties:

    ◊ Resolve disputes.

    ◊ Agree upon courses of action.

    ◊ Bargain for individual or collective advantage.

    ◊ Attempt to craft outcomes that serve their mutual interests.

- Most nurses use negotiation on a daily basis.

- Negotiation may involve the use of several conflict resolution strategies.

- The focus is on a win-win solution or a win/lose-win/lose solution in which both parties win and lose a portion of their original objectives.

    ◊ Each party agrees to give up something and the emphasis is on accommodating differences rather than similarities between parties.

    ◊ For example, one nurse offers to care for Client A today if the other will care for Client B tomorrow.

Δ Communication

- Open communication among staff and between staff and clients can help defray the need for conflict resolution.

- Communication is a two-way process: The sender relays a message to the receiver via a channel (e.g., face to face, telephone, written), and feedback is provided from the receiver and may be context-bound.

Nurse-client relationship	Nurse-health care team relationship
• The goal is to establish a mutually expressive, therapeutic relationship. • Collaborative relationships balance power and respect. • Joint problem solving can often solve problems before they evolve into a conflict.	• The focus is on meeting goals of client care. • Support, guidance, and encouragement among team members can help decrease stressors of the health care environment. • Building positive relationships between coworkers can create a supportive, problem-solving environment, decreasing the incidence of conflict.

- **Assertiveness**

  ◊ Assertive communication allows an individual to express herself in direct, honest, and appropriate ways that do not infringe upon the rights of others.

  ◊ It is a communication style that acknowledges and deals with conflict, recognizes others as equals, and provides a direct statement of feelings.

Δ Grievances

- Conflicts that cannot be satisfactorily resolved may need to be managed by a third party.

- All health care facilities have a grievance policy that should be used when a conflict cannot be resolved or an employee feels he has been unfairly treated.

- The steps of an institution's grievance procedure should be outlined in the grievance policy.

- Typical steps of the grievance process include:

  ◊ Formal presentation of the complaint(s) using the proper chain of command.

  ◊ Formal hearing if the issue is not resolved at a lower level.

  ◊ Professional mediation if a solution is not reached during a formal hearing.

Nursing Interventions

△ **Conflict Resolution Strategies**

Strategy	Characteristics
• Compromising	• Each party gives up something. • To consider this a win-win solution, both parties must give up something equally valuable. If one party gives up more than the other, it can become a win-lose solution.
• Competing	• One party pursues a desired solution at the expense of others. • This is usually a win-lose solution. • Managers may use this when a quick or unpopular decision must be made. • The party who loses something may experience anger, frustration, and a desire for retribution.
• Cooperating/ Accommodating	• One party sacrifices something, allowing the other party to get what it wants. This is the opposite of competing. • This is a lose-win solution. • The original problem may not actually be resolved. • The solution may contribute to future conflict.
• Smoothing	• One party attempts to "smooth" another party, decreasing the emotional component of the conflict. • Often used to preserve or maintain a peaceful work environment. • The focus may be on what is agreed upon, leaving conflict largely unresolved. • This is usually a lose-lose solution.
• Avoiding	• Both parties know there is a conflict, but they refuse to face it or attempt to resolve it. • May be appropriate for minor conflicts or when one party holds more power than the other party or if the issue may work itself out over time. • Since the conflict remains, it may surface again at a later date and escalate over time. • This is usually a lose-lose solution.

Δ   The following example will illustrate a situation using each conflict resolution strategy:

An experienced nurse on a urology unit arrives to work on the night shift. The unit manager immediately asks the nurse to float to a pediatrics unit because the hospital census is high and they are understaffed. The nurse has always maintained a positive attitude when asked to float to medical-surgical units but states she does not feel comfortable in the pediatric setting. The manager insists the nurse is the most qualified.

Compromising	• This approach generally minimizes the losses for all involved while making certain each party gains something. • For example, the nurse might offer to float to another medical-surgical unit if someone from that unit feels comfortable in the pediatric environment. • Although each party is giving up something (i.e., the manager gives in to a different solution and the nurse still has to float), this sort of compromise can result in a win-win resolution.
Competing	• If the nurse truly feels unqualified to float to pediatrics, then this approach may be appropriate – the nurse must win and the manager must lose. • Although risking termination by refusing the assignment, the nurse should take an assertive approach and inform the manager that children would be placed at risk.
Cooperating/ Accommodating	• If the nurse decides to accommodate the manager's request, then the children may be at risk for incompetent care. • Practice liability is another issue for consideration.
Avoiding or Smoothing	• The nurse basically cannot use these strategies since the manager has the power. The conflict cannot be simply avoided or smoothed over; the nurse cannot withdraw from the situation without some sort of negative consequence.

Δ   **Communication Strategies**

•   Use clear, simple, concise verbal communication.

•   Speak directly to the desired receiver. Do not rely on information being transmitted by others.

•   Be an active listener.

•   Observe for nonverbal cues.

Δ Assertiveness Strategies

- Maintain eye contact.

- Convey empathy.

- Speak clearly and audibly, as well as directly and descriptively.

- Use gestures and facial expressions for emphasis.

- Select an appropriate location and time for verbal exchanges.

- Focus on the behavior or issue of conflict; do not make personal attacks.

- Assertive communication with an aggressive client includes:

  ◊ Reflecting the sender's message back to the sender, including the affective element.

  ◊ Pointing out key points and assumptions of the sender's message to demonstrate understanding.

  ◊ Restating the sender's message using assertive rather than aggressive language.

  ◊ Defusing the emotional element and attempting to focus on steps of the problem-solving process using appropriate conflict resolution strategies.

Primary Reference:

Marquis, B. L., & Huston, C. J. (2006). *Leadership roles and management functions in nursing: Theory and application* (5th ed.). Philadelphia: Lippincott Williams & Wilkins.

Additional Resources:

Catalano, J. T. (2003). *Nursing now!: Today's issues, tomorrow's trends* (3rd ed.). Philadelphia: F.A. Davis.

Marquis, B. L. & Huston, C. J. (1998). *Management decision making for nurses: 124 case studies* (3rd ed.). Philadelphia: Lippincott Williams & Wilkins.

Potter, P. A., & Perry, A. G. (2005). *Fundamentals of nursing* (6th ed.). St. Louis, MO: Mosby.

Chapter 8: Conflict Resolution

Application Exercises

1. A nurse is hired to a unit to replace a staff member who has quit. After working on the unit for several weeks, the nurse notices that the unit manager does not intervene when there is conflict between team members, even when it escalates to a high level. Which of the following descriptions best describes the environment the unit manager is sustaining?

   A. An environment that allows open and honest communication

   B. An environment that motivates the team to make changes

   C. An environment that may foster organizational stasis

   D. An environment in which the level of conflict could be demoralizing, anxiety producing, and contribute to burnout

2. Give an example of a conflict in which the win-win conflict resolution strategy of compromise is used.

3. A nurse caring for a client needs to carry out an order for a dressing change on an abdominal wound that has dehisced. The order specifies that the dressing change be done every shift. The client has had visitors in his room all day and has been refusing to allow the nurse to complete the dressing change. Which of the following actions by the nurse would be the most appropriate to use initially?

   A. Assertively tell the client that the dressing must be changed now and the family can wait in the waiting room.

   B. Explain the need for the dressing change and negotiate a time when it can be done.

   C. Delegate the task to the nurse on the next shift.

   D. Invite the visitors to stay while the dressing is being changed.

4. Which of the following statements and behaviors are representative of proper execution of assertive communication? (Select all that apply.)

_____ The focus is on the conflict or issue.

_____ Use of gestures are avoided and facial expressions minimized.

_____ Empathetic statements are used.

_____ The individual is confronted in a public location.

_____ Direct statements of feelings are made.

_____ Eye contact is maintained.

_____ Subjective terms are judiciously used.

5. True or False: Variation in age of health care team members can create organizational conflict.

Chapter 8: Conflict Resolution

Application Exercises Answer Key

1. A nurse is hired to a unit to replace a staff member who has quit. After working on the unit for several weeks, the nurse notices that the unit manager does not intervene when there is conflict between team members, even when it escalates to a high level. Which of the following descriptions best describes the environment the unit manager is sustaining?

   A. An environment that allows open and honest communication
   B. An environment that motivates the team to make changes
   C. An environment that may foster organizational stasis
   D. An environment in which the level of conflict could be demoralizing, anxiety producing, and contribute to burnout

   Environments that support a high level of conflict can be quite demoralizing and anxiety producing, which contributes to burnout. While it is possible that there could be open and honest communication and motivation for change on this unit, the likelihood is undermined by the excessive level of conflict being tolerated by management. Organizational stasis occurs in relation to lack of conflict, not the presence of conflict.

2. Give an example of a conflict in which the win-win conflict resolution strategy of compromise is used.

   Compromise requires that 1) both parties give up something and 2) they give up something equally valuable. The example should include these two elements.

   For instance, two nurses contest their work assignments with the charge nurse. They have both been assigned six clients, a number that is perceived as excessive. A compromise might be for each nurse to take six clients, but the charge nurse also assigns a nurse aide to help the nurses with the 12 clients' basic care.

3. A nurse caring for a client needs to carry out an order for a dressing change on an abdominal wound that has dehisced. The order specifies that the dressing change be done every shift. The client has had visitors in his room all day and has been refusing to allow the nurse to complete the dressing change. Which of the following actions by the nurse would be the most appropriate to use initially?

> A. Assertively tell the client that the dressing must be changed now and the family can wait in the waiting room.
>
> **B. Explain the need for the dressing change and negotiate a time when it can be done.**
>
> C. Delegate the task to the nurse on the next shift.
>
> D. Invite the visitors to stay while the dressing is being changed.

Negotiation of a time to do the dressing change will mutually serve the interests of both the client and the nurse. This should be tried initially, and if it does not resolve the problem the nurse should then approach the client assertively. Delegating the task to the next shift does not maintain the standard of care set by the primary care provider, and inviting the visitors to stay during the dressing change would be an invasion of the client's privacy.

4. Which of the following statements and behaviors are representative of proper execution of assertive communication? (Select all that apply.)

> __X__ **The focus is on the conflict or issue.**
>
> _____ Use of gestures are avoided and facial expressions minimized.
>
> __X__ **Empathetic statements are used.**
>
> _____ The individual is confronted in a public location.
>
> __X__ **Direct statements of feelings are made.**
>
> __X__ **Eye contact is maintained.**
>
> _____ Subjective terms are judiciously used.

Assertive communication allows an individual to express himself in a direct, honest, objective manner that acknowledges the feelings of both parties. The focus is on the conflict or issue, and personal attacks are avoided. Assertive confrontations should be done in a mutually agreed upon place, and the sender of the communication should maintain eye contact with the receiver to ensure that body language and facial expressions of both parties reflect mutual understanding.

5. True or False: Variation in age of health care team members can create organizational conflict.

True: Age is one of the factors that is making the health care environment more diverse. New graduates, who are often younger, are hired to work beside older, more established nurses. A difference in work ethic, personal values, and practice can cause disagreements that can lead to organizational conflict.

Unit 3   Supervisor of Client Care

Chapter 9:   Staff Development and Performance Improvement

Contributors: Rebecca A. Feather, MSN, RN, CNA, BC
Paula Reams, PhD, RN, LMT
Polly Gerber Zimmermann, MS, MBA, RN, CEN, FAEN

 NCLEX® Connections:

Learning Objective: Review and apply knowledge within "**Staff Development and Performance Improvement**" in readiness for performance of the following nursing activities as outlined by the NCLEX® test plans:

Δ   Assess staff's ability to perform assigned tasks; evaluate the results of the care they provide to clients.

Δ   Report unsafe performance by any staff member.

Δ   Identify staff education needs, participate in staff education, and evaluate the outcomes of staff education.

Δ   Identify and report client care issues for performance improvement.

Δ   Engage in and evaluate the outcome (impact on client care and resource use) of performance improvement activities.

 Key Points

Δ   **Staff Development**

- The quality of client care provided is directly related to the education and level of competency of health care providers.

- Development is intended to enhance the competence of all staff and to help them meet standards set forth by the facility and accrediting bodies.

- Needs for staff development should be brought to the attention of appropriate educative personnel.

- Development may be provided by peers, unit managers, and staff development educators, utilizing methods appropriate to the learning domain and staff learning styles.

- **Indoctrination and socialization**

  ◊ **Indoctrination** is the process by which a person is taught the beliefs or ideology of a culture without discouraging independent thought.

  ◊ **Socialization** is the process by which a person learns the values and culture of a new setting.

  ◊ Successful indoctrination and socialization helps new staff members fit in with already established staff on a client care unit.

  ◊ Staff development educators and unit managers may begin this process during interviewing and orientation.

  ◊ Nurse preceptors are frequently used to assist new nurses with this task on the clinical unit.

- **Orientation**

  ◊ Helps new graduates translate knowledge, principles, skills, and theories learned in nursing school into practice.

  ◊ Is necessary for nurses new to a health care facility or unit to learn the procedures and protocols.

- **Competence**

  ◊ Is the ability to meet the requirement of a particular role.

  ◊ Strategies to maintain competence include:

    ° Use of checklists to provide a record of opportunities and the level of proficiency in relation to skills.

    ° Peer observation/evaluation, planned or incidental, to assess competence.

    ° Completion of electronic learning modules.

    ° Attendance at in-services to update skills.

    ° Attendance at training sessions to learn specialized skills (Advanced Cardiac Life Support, Pediatric Life Support).

Δ **Performance Improvement**

- Performance improvement (e.g., quality improvement, quality control) is the process used to identify and resolve performance deficiencies.

- Performance improvement includes measuring performance against a set of predetermined standards. In health care these standards may be set by the specific facility and take into consideration accrediting and professional standards.

- The Joint Commission (formerly JCAHO):

  ◊ Sets standards in relation to policies, procedures, and the competency of health care team members.

  ◊ Annually publishes the National Patient Safety Goals (NPSGs), which specify the standard of care that clients should receive.

  ◊ Requirements include:

    ° Policies, procedures, and standards describe and guide how the nursing staff provides nursing care, treatment, and services.

    ° All nursing policies, procedures, and standards are defined, documented, and accessible in written or electronic format.

Key Procedural Points

Δ **Staff Development**

- Evaluation of staff development includes:

  ◊ Use of evaluative materials, observations, and review audits to measure behavior change.

  ◊ Identifying evidence of behavior change (e.g., demonstration of desired level of proficiency, decrease in medication errors).

  ◊ Providing further orientation/training to meet staff development needs.

Δ **Performance Improvement**

- Step 1

  ◊ Standard is developed and approved by facility committee.

- Step 2

  ◊ Provide and document care according to the developed standard.

  ◊ An audit is performed to determine if the standard is being met.

Timing of Audits	Types of Audits
• **Retrospective audit** occurs after the client receives care. • **Concurrent audit** occurs while the client is receiving care. • **Prospective audit** predicts how future client care will be affected by current level of services.	• **Structure audits** evaluate the influence of elements that exist separate from or outside of the client-staff interaction. • **Process audits** review how care was provided and assume a relationship exists between the nurse and the quality of care provided. • **Outcome audits** determine what results, if any, occurred as a result of the nursing care provided.

- Step 3

  ◊ Educational or corrective action is provided when results indicate that a standard is not being met.

The Nurse's Role in Performance Improvement	
Step	**Interventions**
Step 1	• Serve as unit representative on committees developing policies and procedures. • Use reliable resources for information (e.g., Centers for Disease Control and Prevention, professional journals, evidenced-based research).
Step 2	• Enhance knowledge and understanding of the facility's policies and procedures. • Provide client care consistent with these policies and procedures. • Document client care thoroughly and according to facility guidelines. • Participate in the collection of information/data related to staff's adherence to selected policy or procedure. • Assist with analysis of the information/data. • Compare results with the established standard. • Make a judgment about performance in regard to the findings.
Step 3	• Assist with provision of education or training necessary to improve the performance of staff. • Act as a role model by practicing in accordance with the established standard. • Assist with re-evaluation of staff performance by collection of information/data at a specified time.

Primary Reference:

Marquis, B. L., & Huston, C. J. (2006). *Leadership roles and management functions in nursing: Theory and application* (5th ed.). Philadelphia: Lippincott Williams & Wilkins.

Additional Resources:

Abruzzese, R. S. (1996). *Nursing staff development: Strategies for success* (2nd ed.). St. Louis, MO: Mosby.

The Joint Commission. (n.d.). *The Joint Commission.* Retrieved April 4, 2007, at http://www.jointcommission.org/

Chapter 9: Staff Development and Performance Improvement

Application Exercises

1. As a part of orientation for new graduates, which of the following educational foci should be included? (Select all that apply.)

    _____ Skill proficiency

    _____ Assignment to a preceptor

    _____ Budgetary principles

    _____ Computerized charting

    _____ Socialization into unit culture

    _____ Facility policies and procedures

2. A new graduate nurse witnesses an established nurse documenting an assessment of a patient controlled analgesia (PCA) pump incorrectly on the computerized flow sheet. Which of the following should the new graduate nurse do?

    A. Notify the charge nurse that the nurse has a staff development need.

    B. Leave a note for the unit manager that established staff may have a learning need in regard to computerized charting.

    C. Bring to the nurse's attention that she is charting incorrectly and offer to demonstrate proper charting on the flow sheet.

    D. Question her own level of proficiency and seek out her preceptor for verification of correct procedure.

3. At the end of a staff in-service training on the use of a new piece of equipment for lifting clients, what must be done to determine if knowledge acquisition occurred?

4. A new IV pump is being introduced on an oncology unit. A medical distributor representative has just provided a demonstration of the new pump. Describe what strategies the unit manager can use to ensure that staff can properly and safely use the new pumps.

5. Performance improvement primarily endeavors to identify if which of the following are being met?

        A. Outcomes

        B. Standards

        C. Performance indicators

        D. Procedural guidelines

6. An audit that is done while a client is receiving care is called which of the following?

        A. Retrospective

        B. Concurrent

        C. Prospective

        D. Process

7. The unit manager of a surgical unit receives a memo from the risk management department. The memo is in reference to an excessive number of incident reports related to medication errors involving omission of a dose of antibiotics. The unit manager brings this issue to the attention of staff at the monthly staff meeting. A new graduate who had a degree in business prior to becoming a nurse volunteers to do an audit as a part of a quarterly performance improvement strategic plan. What type of audit would be most effective, how should the new graduate structure the audit, and who should be involved?

Chapter 9: Staff Development and Performance Improvement

Application Exercises Answer Key

1. As a part of orientation for new graduates, which of the following educational foci should be included? (Select all that apply.)

   __X__ **Skill proficiency**

   __X__ **Assignment to a preceptor**

   _____ Budgetary principles

   __X__ **Computerized charting**

   __X__ **Socialization into unit culture**

   __X__ **Facility policies and procedures**

   All of the above except budgetary principles need to be included in the orientation of new graduates. They need support in relation to transitioning to their first job as well as becoming socialized into their new unit's culture. Budgetary principles are a higher level administrative skill that is usually the responsibility of the unit manager.

2. A new graduate nurse witnesses an established nurse documenting an assessment of a patient controlled analgesia (PCA) pump incorrectly on the computerized flow sheet. Which of the following should the new graduate nurse do?

   A. Notify the charge nurse that the nurse has a staff development need.

   B. Leave a note for the unit manager that established staff may have a learning need in regard to computerized charting.

   C. **Bring to the nurse's attention that she is charting incorrectly and offer to demonstrate proper charting on the flow sheet.**

   D. Question her own level of proficiency and seek out her preceptor for verification of correct procedure.

   It is every nurse's responsibility to observe for and report or correct unsafe practices. Even though the nurse is a new graduate, if the skill observed is within her purview of practice, she has the responsibility to attempt to correct and educate the nurse in relation to proper charting. If the nurse is not open to her interventions, then the new graduate nurse should speak with the unit manager regarding her concerns.

3. At the end of a staff in-service training on the use of a new piece of equipment for lifting clients, what must be done to determine if knowledge acquisition occurred?

It is important to evaluate what learning took place. Various methods may be used. Immediate recall can be evaluated by the use of a multiple choice quiz and return demonstration of proper equipment use. Long-term recall can be evaluated by direct observation of staff use of equipment. Follow-up training should be provided if adequate learning did not take place.

4. A new IV pump is being introduced on an oncology unit. A medical distributor representative has just provided a demonstration of the new pump. Describe what strategies the unit manager can use to ensure that staff can properly and safely use the new pumps.

Give the staff opportunities to practice with the pump in a laboratory or nonclinical setting.
Use a skill checklist to guide the nurses through the learning process.
Have the nurses perform a return demonstration of the skill.
Follow up training with future observations.

5. Performance improvement primarily endeavors to identify if which of the following are being met?

A. Outcomes
B. Standards
C. Performance indicators
D. Procedural guidelines

While all of the above are focused on at some point during performance improvement, the primary endeavor of performance improvement is to determine if standards set by the institution are being met.

6. An audit that is done while a client is receiving care is called which of the following?

    A. Retrospective

    B. Concurrent

    C. Prospective

    D. Process

A concurrent audit is done while the client is still receiving care. A retrospective audit is done after client care; a prospective audit is done in anticipation of care; and a process audit is done to review how care was provided and what relationship exists between the nurse and quality of care provided.

7. The unit manager of a surgical unit receives a memo from the risk management department. The memo is in reference to an excessive number of incident reports related to medication errors involving omission of a dose of antibiotics. The unit manager brings this issue to the attention of staff at the monthly staff meeting. A new graduate who had a degree in business prior to becoming a nurse volunteers to do an audit as a part of a quarterly performance improvement strategic plan. What type of audit would be most effective, how should the new graduate structure the audit, and who should be involved?

A retrospective process audit would allow the protocol for medication administration to be evaluated in relation to compliance with the standardized guidelines. The new graduate should ask for staff volunteers who would like to help with the audit to develop a team of auditors. First, the protocol that outlines the standard of care expected for medication administration should be reviewed. Second, records of clients who had a medication error should be reviewed, using a checklist of predetermined criteria to analyze each error (e.g., shift, type of medication, reason for error). Third, using the results of the audit as data, a comparison should be made with the protocol to determine if it was being followed or if the errors were a result of noncompliance with institutional protocol. If this is found to be true, the report should make recommendations, such as provision of staff education. After staff education has been implemented, another audit should be done at a specified time (e.g., 6 months later) to re-evaluate staff performance.

Unit 3   Supervisor of Client Care

Chapter 10:	Time Management

Contributors: Annette C. Milius, MA, RN, APRN-BC
                   Polly Gerber Zimmermann, MS, MBA, RN, CEN, FAEN

 NCLEX® Connections:

Learning Objective: Review and apply knowledge within "**Time Management**" in readiness for performance of the following nursing activities as outlined by the NCLEX® test plans:

Δ   Use effective time management skills in the provision and direction of client care.

Δ   Monitor the effectiveness of personal time management skills and the effectiveness of other staff members' time management skills.

 Key Points

Δ   **Time Management**

•   Time management is the art of making the best use of time available to achieve specific tasks.

Good time management	Poor time management
Facilitates greater productivity. Decreases work-related stress. Helps ensure the provision of quality and appropriately prioritized client care. Decreases burnout by increasing personal and professional satisfaction.	Leads to feelings of being overwhelmed and stressed. Creates dissatisfaction with care provided. Increases the omission of important tasks. Results in errors.

•   **Time Wasters**

◊   Socializing

◊   Poor planning/management by crisis

◊   Reluctance to delegate/underdelegation

◊   Missing equipment when preparing to perform a procedure

◊   Low level of skill proficiency, increasing time on task

◊   Procrastination

- **Priority Setting** (*Refer to chapter 6, Prioritizing Client Care.*)

    ◊ Involves decision making regarding the order in which:

    ° Clients are seen.

    ° Assessments are completed.

    ° Interventions are provided.

    ° Steps in a client procedure are completed.

    ° Components of client care are completed.

Key Procedural Points

Δ **Time management** is a cyclic process.

- Take the time to plan. Set goals and plan care based on established priorities and thoughtful utilization of resources. Time initially spent developing a plan will save time later and help to avoid management by crisis.

- Complete one client care task before beginning the next, starting with the highest priority task.

- Reprioritize remaining tasks based on continual reassessment of client care needs.

- The most common mistake is NOT taking the time to develop a plan for care.

Nursing Interventions

Δ **Time Management for Client Care**

- Assess client needs and activities.

- Analyze resources.

- Develop a plan that makes the best use of time and resources to meet client care objectives.

- Use time savers.

    ◊ Mentally envision the procedure to be performed and ensure all equipment has been gathered prior to entering the client's room.

    ◊ Group activities that are to be performed on the same client or are in close physical proximity to prevent unnecessary walking.

    ◊ Estimate how long each activity will take and plan accordingly.

◊ Document nursing interventions as soon as possible after completion to facilitate accurate and thorough documentation.

◊ Delegate activities to other staff when client care workload is beyond what can be managed by one nurse.

◊ Enlist the aid of other staff when a team approach would be more efficient than an individual approach.

◊ Complete more difficult or strenuous tasks when energy level is high.

◊ Avoid interruptions and graciously but assertively say "no" to unreasonable or poorly timed requests for help.

◊ Set a realistic standard for completion of care and level of performance.

◊ Complete one task before beginning another task.

◊ Avoid procrastination – break large tasks into smaller tasks.

◊ Use an organizational sheet to plan out care.

◊ Minimize distractions and interruptions.

• Minimize socializing.

◊ Keep communication focused and professional.

◊ Use breaks and pre/post shift time for personal socializing.

◊ Upon entering the client's room, state purpose and tasks to be completed.

◊ If the client wishes to socialize, the nurse should politely excuse herself and explain that she will return later.

Δ **Time Management and Team Work**

• Be cognizant of assistance needed by other health care team members.

• Offer to help when unexpected crises occur.

• Assist other team members with provision of care when experiencing a period of "down time."

Δ **Time Management and the Nursing Process**

• Ensure necessary time is made available to:

◊ Assess.

◊ Plan care.

◊ Coordinate care with other health care team members.

◊ Evaluate the effectiveness of efforts and the plan of care.

• Enhance the proficiency level of technical skills to decrease time wasted.

Δ   **Time Management and Self-Care**

- Take time for oneself.

- Schedule time for breaks and meals.

- Take physical and mental breaks from work/unit.

Δ   **Priority Setting**

- Determine:

    ◊   What needs to be done **immediately** (e.g., administration of analgesic or antiemetic, assessment of an unstable client).

    ◊   What needs to be completed by a **specific time** to ensure client safety, quality care, and compliance with facility policies and procedures (e.g., medication administration, vital signs, blood glucose monitoring).

    ◊   What must be done by the **end of the shift** (e.g., ambulation of the client, discharge and/or discharge teaching, dressing change).

    ◊   What can be delegated. First determine:

        °   What can be done only by an RN?

        °   What client care responsibilities can be delegated to other health care team members, such as licensed practical nurses (LPNs) and assistive personnel (AP).

        °   How can scheduled client care activities most efficiently be shared by these two groups of care providers?

Primary Reference:

Marquis, B. L., & Huston, C. J. (2006). *Leadership roles and management functions in nursing: Theory and application* (5th ed.). Philadelphia: Lippincott Williams & Wilkins.

Additional Resources:

Marquis, B. L. & Huston, C. J. (1998). *Management decision making for nurses: 124 case studies* (3rd ed.). Philadelphia: Lippincott Williams & Wilkins.

Chapter 10: Time Management

Application Exercises

1. The most common mistake unit-based nurses make in regard to time management is

    A. prioritizing poorly.

    B. not using the nursing process.

    C. failing to delegate.

    D. not taking the time to plan.

2. Which of the following may occur due to poor time management? (Select all that apply.)

    _____ Feeling overwhelmed

    _____ Being stressed

    _____ Frequent errors

    _____ Satisfaction with quality of care provided

    _____ Greater productivity

3. A nurse is preparing to insert an intravenous catheter in a client who also needs to receive morphine sulfate 10 mg IV push. Using time management principles, number the following steps in the order in which the nurse should perform them.

    _____ Mentally envision the procedure when collecting supplies.

    _____ Enter the room and wash hands.

    _____ Draw up morphine sulfate and plan to administer immediately after IV is established.

    _____ Explain the procedure and prepare the client.

    _____ Notify staff members that she will be unavailable until the task is completed.

4. Which of the following is an appropriate basis upon which to make initial decisions related to delegation of client care activities?

    A. The nurse should assume that since he is accountable for the care his clients receive, he is also responsible for carrying out that care.

    B. The nurse should delegate all possible client care to other levels of providers assigned to his clients (e.g., LPNs, AP).

    C. The nurse should collaborate with other levels of providers assigned to his clients and delegate care based on personal preference.

    D. The nurse should retain the client care activities that only an RN can perform and delegate other activities as appropriate.

5. True or False: An important part of efficient time management includes scheduling time for breaks and lunch.

6. True or False: The nursing process is a tool that can be used to help guide a nurse in the planning and coordination of care for multiple clients.

Chapter 10: Time Management

Application Exercises Answer Key

1. The most common mistake unit-based nurses make in regard to time management is

        A. prioritizing poorly.

        B. not using the nursing process.

        C. failing to delegate.

        D. not taking the time to plan.

        Not taking the time to plan is the most common mistake unit-based nurses make. While the other options also contribute to poor time management, the nurse must take the time to plan or she may find herself "managing by crisis."

2. Which of the following may occur due to poor time management? (Select all that apply.)

        __X__ **Feeling overwhelmed**

        __X__ **Being stressed**

        __X__ **Frequent errors**

        _____ Satisfaction with quality of care provided

        _____ Greater productivity

        Poor time management can lead to the occurrence of errors and feelings of being overwhelmed and stressed. Poor time management does not generally lead to satisfaction with the quality of care given and productivity; rather, it can create extremely negative feelings and a sense that substandard care is being given.

3. A nurse is preparing to insert an intravenous catheter in a client who also needs to receive morphine sulfate 10 mg IV push. Using time management principles, number the following steps in the order in which the nurse should perform them.

   __2__   Mentally envision the procedure when collecting supplies.

   __4__   Enter the room and wash hands.

   __3__   Draw up morphine sulfate and plan to administer immediately after IV is established.

   __5__   Explain the procedure and prepare the client.

   __1__   Notify staff members that she will be unavailable until the task is completed.

Step	Rationale
Notify staff members.	Avoiding interruptions will help the nurse to stay focused and complete the task in a timely manner.
Collect supplies.	Mentally envisioning a procedure can help prevent omission of necessary equipment.
Draw up morphine.	The morphine should be drawn up right before entering the room to prevent errors.
Enter room and wash hands.	The next step is to go into the client's room and wash hands in preparation for completing the task.
Explain procedure and prepare the client.	The nurse has completed all preparation steps and is ready to start insertion of the IV.

4. Which of the following is an appropriate basis upon which to make initial decisions related to delegation of client care activities?

    A. The nurse should assume that since he is accountable for the care his clients receive, he is also responsible for carrying out that care.

    B. The nurse should delegate all possible client care to other levels of providers assigned to his clients (e.g., LPNs, AP).

    C. The nurse should collaborate with other levels of providers assigned to his clients and delegate care based on personal preference.

    D. The nurse should retain the client care activities that only an RN can perform and delegate other activities as appropriate.

The nurse should begin the process of delegation by determining what he alone can do relative to his role as a professional nurse and team leader. While the nurse retains accountability for the care his clients receive, the nurse usually does not have the time to carry out all activities and should delegate selected responsibilities to other health care team members. However, the nurse may not want to delegate all possible care to other levels of providers, since this would significantly decrease client contact and informed care planning. After the nurse determines what he would like to delegate, these activities can then be distributed based on appropriate delegation guidelines.

5. True or False: An important part of efficient time management includes scheduling time for breaks and lunch.

True: It is very important for the nurse to take time for himself, because providing client care is a very mentally and physically demanding job.

6. True or False: The nursing process is a tool that can be used to help guide a nurse in the planning and coordination of care for multiple clients.

True: The steps of the nursing process can be applied to planning and coordinating client care. The nurse must first assess clients' care needs and resources available, plan care accordingly with team members, coordinate and supervise care provided by the team, and then evaluate the effectiveness and quality of care provided.

Unit 4   Collaborator/Planner of Client Care

Chapter 11:   Disaster Planning and Emergency Management
Contributor: Annette C. Milius, MA, RN, APRN-BC

 NCLEX® Connections:

Learning Objective: Review and apply knowledge within "**Disaster Planning and Emergency Management**" in readiness for performance of the following nursing activities as outlined by the NCLEX® test plans:

Δ   Engage in disaster and emergency management planning activities, including planning for discharge of clients as appropriate.

Δ   Respond to internal and external emergencies per emergency response plan.

Δ   Follow procedures for evacuation of clients as appropriate.

 Key Points

Δ   **Disaster Planning and Emergency Management**

- A disaster is an event that overwhelms, at least temporarily, the capacity of a hospital.

- Mass casualties overwhelm the resources of individual hospitals and possibly the resources of the community's entire health care system.

  ◊   A prompt local response is essential to emergency management. Assistance from regional, state, and federal agencies may follow.

- Internal emergencies include loss of electric power or potable water and severe damage or casualties within the facility related to fire, severe weather (e.g., tornado, hurricane), an explosion, or a terrorist act.

  ◊   Internal emergency readiness includes safety and hazardous materials procedures and infection control policies and practices.

- External emergencies include hurricanes, floods, volcano eruptions, earthquakes, pandemic flu, chemical plant explosions, industrial accidents, building collapse, major transportation accidents, and terrorist acts (including biological and chemical warfare).

  ◊   External emergency readiness includes a plan to participate in community-wide emergencies and disasters.

- The Joint Commission (formerly JCAHO) establishes emergency preparedness management standards for health care facilities (e.g., long-term care, behavioral health care, critical access hospitals). These standards include procedures for:

  ◊ Notifying and assigning personnel.

  ◊ Notifying external authorities of emergencies.

  ◊ Managing space and supplies and providing security.

  ◊ Radioactive or chemical isolation and decontamination (e.g., measures to contain contamination, decontamination at scene of exposure).

  ◊ Evacuation and setting up an alternative care site when the environment cannot support adequate client care and treatment. Critical processes when an alternative care site is necessary include:

    ° Client packaging (medications, admissions, medical records, and tracking).

    ° Interfacility communication.

    ° Transportation of clients, staff, and equipment.

    ° Cross-privileging of medical staff.

  ◊ Triage of incoming clients.

  ◊ Management of clients during emergencies, including scheduling, modification or discontinuation of services, control of client information, and client transportation.

  ◊ Interaction with family members and the news media.

  ◊ Identification of backup resources (electricity, water, fire protection, fuel sources, medical gas and vacuum) for utilities and communication.

  ◊ Orientation and education of personnel who will participate in implementation of the emergency preparedness plan.

  ◊ Crisis support for health care workers (access to vaccines, infection control advice, mental health counseling).

  ◊ Performance monitoring and evaluation related to emergency preparedness.

  ◊ Conducting two emergency preparedness drills each year.

    ° Drills should include an influx of clients beyond those being treated by the facility.

    ° Drills should include either an internal or an external disaster (i.e., a situation beyond the normal capacity of the facility).

Community Preparedness

Δ **Community-wide preparedness** includes:

- Development and daily testing of a community-wide communication network.

- Maintaining an inventory of capabilities and resources within the community.

- Participation in community-wide mass casualty drills.

- Pre-arrangement of supervision, shelter, and food for the families and pets of those who will be working in response to a disaster.

- Determining the capacity of each health care facility within the community, including the:

  ◊ Availability of beds.

  ◊ Number of trained staff (best indicator of the capacity of the health system to respond to mass casualty incidents).

- Calculating an unduplicated estimate of the number and sources of additional staff.

  ◊ Identifying and regularly training "reserve staff" – physicians, nurses, and hospital workers who are retired, have changed careers, or are working in areas other than direct client care; and possibly medical, nursing, and allied health students training in programs affiliated with the health care facility.

- Stockpiling supplies based on "anticipated" potential needs.

- Establishing a plan for external and internal communications. This plan should include:

  ◊ A single community site for obtaining patient locator information (e.g., Red Cross).

  ◊ A communication center away from health care facilities at which a single regional spokesperson will provide information to media at pre-announced media briefing times.

- Ensuring open channels of communication with emergency response teams (backup methods as needed).

- Maintaining a current list of personnel and emergency telephone numbers.

- Planning for crowd control (e.g., photo ID cards for staff, identification for reserve staff) to ease ability to cross crowd control perimeter.

- Planning to maintain clients' privacy and right to confidentiality.
  - ◊ Do not provide client information without informed consent of clients.
  - ◊ Do not release the identity of accident victims until all family members have been notified.
- Planning for the evacuation of clients.
  - ◊ Evacuate clients as needed in order to:
    - ° Remove clients and personnel from actual or threatened danger.
    - ° Free hospital beds for the care of incoming casualties.
  - ◊ Perform roll call before, during, and after evacuation, if possible.
- Planning for the discharge of hospitalized clients.
  - ◊ Empty beds are used first, routine admissions are cancelled, and then the following types of clients are discharged as needed until enough bed space is made to handle the influx of casualties.
    - ° Clients who are hospitalized for diagnosis or observation and are not bedridden
    - ° Clients who were already close to being discharged
    - ° Postnatal clients and babies after 24 hr

Nursing Interventions

Δ Triage

- Separate casualties and allocate treatment based on victims' potential for survival.
  - ◊ Highest priority is given to clients with life-threatening injuries but a high possibility of survival once stabilized.
  - ◊ Second highest priority is given to clients who have injuries that involve systemic complications that are not yet life threatening and can usually wait 45 to 60 min for treatment.
  - ◊ Lowest priority is given to clients who have local injuries with no immediate complications and can usually wait several hours for treatment.

Δ **Fire**

- The **RACE** mnemonic is a basic guideline for reacting to a fire within the health care facility.

Rescue	• **Rescue** everyone from the area.
Alarm	• Pull the fire **alarm**, which will activate the EMS response. • Systems that could increase fire spread are automatically shut down with activation of the alarm.
Contain	• Once the room or area has been cleared, the fire doors should be kept closed in order to **contain** the fire. • Keep fire doors closed as much as possible when moving from section to section within the facility.
Extinguish	• Make an attempt to **extinguish** small fires using a single fire extinguisher, smothering, or water (except with an electrical or grease fire). • Evacuation should occur if the nurse cannot put the fire out with these methods. • Attempts at extinguishing the fire should only be made when the employee has been properly trained in the safe and proper use of a fire extinguisher and when only one extinguisher is needed.

Δ **Severe Thunderstorm/Tornado**

- Draw all shades and close all drapes as protection against shattering glass.

- Lower all beds to the lowest position and move beds away from the windows.

- Place blankets on all clients who are confined to beds.

- Close all doors.

- Get as many ambulatory clients as possible into the hallways (away from windows).

- Do not use elevators.

- Turn the weather radio unit on for severe weather warnings.

- Follow instructions from the unit manager.

Δ **Biological Incidents**

- Take measures to protect self and others.

- Have knowledge of which facilities are open to exposed clients and which are only open to unexposed clients.

- Participate in community-wide surveillance and identification of a pattern among apparently isolated incidents.

- Recognize signs and symptoms of infection/poisoning and appropriate treatment.

Incident	Signs and Symptoms	Treatment/Prevention
Inhalational anthrax	• Sore throat • Fever • Muscle aches • Severe dyspnea • Meningitis • Shock	• IV ciprofloxacin (Cipro)
Botulism	• Difficulty swallowing • Progressive weakness • Nausea, vomiting, and abdominal cramps • Difficulty breathing	• Airway management • Antitoxin • Elimination of toxin
Smallpox	• High fever • Fatigue • Severe headache • Rash (starts centrally and spreads outward) that turns to pus-filled lesions • Vomiting • Delirium • Excessive bleeding	• Treatment: No cure • Supportive care: Hydration, pain medication, antipyretics • Prevention: Vaccine
Ebola	• Sore throat • Headache • High temperature • Nausea, vomiting, diarrhea • Internal and external bleeding • Shock	• Treatment: No cure • Supportive care: Minimize invasive procedures • Prevention: Vaccine

Δ   **Chemical Incidents**

- Assess and intervene to maintain the client's airway, breathing, and circulation.

- Effectively remove the offending chemical by undressing the client, removing all identifiable particulate matter, and providing immediate and prolonged irrigations of contaminated areas.

- Gather a specific history of the injury, if possible (e.g., name and concentration of the chemical, duration of exposure, previous client history).

- In the event of chemical warfare, have knowledge of which facilities are open to exposed clients and which are only open to unexposed clients.

- Follow the facility's emergency management plans (e.g., for personal protection measures, the handling and disposal of wastes, use of space and equipment, reporting procedures).

Δ   Hazardous Material Incidents

- Take measures to protect self and to avoid contact.

- Approach the scene with caution.

- Attempt to identify the hazardous material (e.g., emergency response guidebook, poison control centers).

- Try to contain the material as much as possible in one place.

- If individuals are contaminated, try decontaminating them as much as possible at the scene or as close as possible to the scene.

  ◊ With few exceptions, water is the universal antidote. For biological hazardous materials, use bleach.

  ◊ Wear gloves, gown, mask, and shoe covers to protect self from contamination.

  ◊ If clothing is contaminated, remove it carefully and slowly so that deposited material does not become airborne.

  ◊ Place all contaminated material into large plastic bags and seal them.

  ◊ Cleanse skin with gentle soap and water. Do not use an abrasive scrub or strong detergent; do not shave hairy areas if there is redness or tenderness.

Δ   Radiological Incidents

- Provide appropriate interventions for radioactively exposed and/or contaminated victims.

- Take appropriate measures to protect self from ionizing radiation when caring for contaminated victims.

Δ   Bomb Threat

- When a phone call is received:

  ◊ Prolong the conversation as long as possible.

  ◊ Be alert for distinguishing background noises, such as music, voices, aircraft, and church bells.

  ◊ Note distinguishing voice characteristics.

  ◊ Ask where the bomb will explode and at what time.

  ◊ Note if the caller indicates knowledge of the facility by his or her description of the location.

- If what appears to be a bomb is found, do not touch it, clear the area, and obtain professional assistance. Try to isolate the object as much as possible by closing doors.

- Notify authorities and key personnel (e.g., police, administrator, director of nursing or supervisor).

- Cooperate with police and others – assist to conduct search as needed, provide copies of floor plans, have master keys available, and watch for and isolate suspicious objects such as packages and boxes.

- Keep elevators available for authorities.

- Remain calm and alert and try not to alarm clients.

Primary Reference:

Marquis, B. L., & Huston, C. J. (2006). *Leadership roles and management functions in nursing: Theory and application* (5th ed.). Philadelphia: Lippincott Williams & Wilkins.

Additional Resources:

Centers for Disease Control and Prevention. (n.d.). *Emergency preparedness & response.* Retrieved January 24, 2007, from http://www.bt.cdc.gov/

American Hospital Association. (n.d.). *Emergency readiness.* Retrieved January 24, 2007, from http://www.aha.org/aha_app/issues/Emergency-Readiness/index.jsp

Stanhope, M. & Lancaster, J. (2006). *Foundations of nursing in the community* (2nd ed.). St. Louis, MO: Mosby.

The Joint Commission. (n.d.). *The Joint Commission.* Retrieved April 4, 2007, at http://www.jointcommission.org/

Chapter 11: Disaster Planning and Emergency Management

Application Exercises

1. A nurse is appointed to a committee to prepare a plan to deal with a weather emergency that could isolate the facility from its usual suppliers and supports. What questions should the nurse and the committee address?

2. A community experiences an outbreak of meningitis, and hospital beds are urgently needed. Which of the following clients is the most appropriate to discharge in order to make room?

   A. 58-year-old man admitted this morning with unstable angina and a history of CABG 1 year ago

   B. 50-year-old adult newly diagnosed with type 2 diabetes mellitus being admitted for minor surgery

   C. 70-year-old adult admitted yesterday with pneumonia and severe dehydration

   D. 55-year-old woman who fell and broke her hip and is scheduled for total hip replacement tomorrow

3. Which of the following levels of government should be the first line of defense in the event of an external disaster?

   A. Local

   B. Regional

   C. State

   D. Federal

4. Which of the following nursing actions are appropriate if a severe weather alarm is activated? (Select all that apply.)

_____ Draw all shades and close all drapes as protection against shattering glass.

_____ Lower all beds to the lowest position and move beds away from the windows as much as possible.

_____ Keep doors open to facilitate quick evacuation of clients.

_____ Get as many ambulatory clients as possible into the hallways.

_____ Use the elevators to move clients to lower levels.

_____ Turn the weather radio unit on for severe weather warnings.

5. A nurse enters a client's room and finds that a fire has started. Number the following actions in the appropriate order in which the nurse should take them.

_____ Close the fire doors on the unit.

_____ Move the client away from the fire.

_____ Activate the fire alarm.

_____ Extinguish the fire (if trained in using a fire extinguisher).

Chapter 11: Disaster Planning and Emergency Management

Application Exercises Answer Key

1. A nurse is appointed to a committee to prepare a plan to deal with a weather emergency that could isolate the facility from its usual suppliers and supports. What questions should the nurse and the committee address?

    Δ   **What sort of backup communication system is in place?**

        •   **Within the facility (walkie talkies?), communication with the outside world (cell phones, pagers?)**

        •   **How would computers function?**

    Δ   **Is there a backup generator for power (lights, heat, and refrigeration)?**

        •   **What would not function using this type of power source?**

        •   **Will clients on mechanical supports be stable?**

    Δ   **What sort of routine supplies are on hand (e.g., food, water, oxygen, medications, tubing, bandages)? How long would they last?**

    Δ   **Can additional staff get to the facility? How should human resources be allocated to accomplish client care tasks?**

2. A community experiences an outbreak of meningitis, and hospital beds are urgently needed. Which of the following clients is the most appropriate to discharge in order to make room?

    A. 58-year-old man admitted this morning with unstable angina and a history of CABG 1 year ago

    B. 50-year-old adult newly diagnosed with type 2 diabetes mellitus being admitted for minor surgery

    C. 70-year-old adult admitted yesterday with pneumonia and severe dehydration

    D. 55-year-old woman who fell and broke her hip and is scheduled for total hip replacement tomorrow

The client newly diagnosed with type 2 diabetes mellitus is the most stable client and would be the most able to continue treatment on an outpatient basis with education and support.

3. Which of the following levels of government should be the first line of defense in the event of an external disaster?

> **A. Local**
> B. Regional
> C. State
> D. Federal

A prompt local response is essential to emergency management. Assistance from regional, state, and federal agencies may follow.

4. Which of the following nursing actions are appropriate if a severe weather alarm is activated? (Select all that apply.)

> __X__ **Draw all shades and close all drapes as protection against shattering glass.**
> __X__ **Lower all beds to the lowest position and move beds away from the windows as much as possible.**
> _____ Keep doors open to facilitate quick evacuation of clients.
> __X__ **Get as many ambulatory clients as possible into the hallways.**
> _____ Use the elevators to move clients to lower levels.
> __X__ **Turn the weather radio unit on for severe weather warnings.**

Measures such as drawing the shades, closing drapes, moving beds away from the window, and moving ambulatory clients into the hallway to protect them from shattering glass are appropriate. Doors should be kept closed and elevator use should be avoided.

5. A nurse enters a client's room and finds that a fire has started. Number the following actions in the appropriate order in which the nurse should take them.

> __3__ Close the fire doors on the unit.
> __1__ Move the client away from the fire.
> __2__ Activate the fire alarm.
> __4__ Extinguish the fire (if trained in using a fire extinguisher).

RACE: Rescue, Alarm, Confine, and Extinguish
Remove everyone from the area.
Pull the fire alarm, which will activate the EMS response.
Once the room or area has been cleared, the fire doors should be kept closed in order to confine the fire.
An attempt to extinguish the fire using a single fire extinguisher can be made only when practical and only when an employee has been properly trained in the safe and proper use of a fire extinguisher.

Unit 4   Collaborator/Planner of Client Care

Chapter 12:   Referrals, Consultations, and Collaboration with the Interdisciplinary Team

Contributors: Annette C. Milius, MA, RN, APRN-BC
Paula Reams, PhD, RN, LMT

 NCLEX® Connections:

Learning Objective: Review and apply knowledge within "**Referrals, Consultations, and Collaboration with the Interdisciplinary Team**" in readiness for performance of the following nursing activities as outlined by the NCLEX® test plans:

Δ   Assess the need for and initiate client referrals for assistance with actual or potential problems.

Δ   Identify community resources for client referrals.

Δ   Provide appropriate documentation with client referrals.

Δ   Assess the need to consult with other health care providers to meet identified client needs and to plan client care.

Δ   Assess the need for and collaborate in the development of interdisciplinary client care plans.

Δ   Communicate information regarding the client's status to members of the interdisciplinary team as needed.

 Key Points

Δ   **Consultations**

- A consultant is a professional who provides expert advice in a particular area. A consultation is requested to help determine what treatment/services the client requires.

- Consultants provide expertise to clients who require a particular type of knowledge or service (e.g., a cardiologist for a client who had a myocardial infarction, a psychiatrist for a client whose risk for suicide needs to be assessed).

- Coordination of the consultant's recommendations with other health care providers' recommendations is necessary to protect the client from conflicting and potentially dangerous orders.

Δ   **Referrals**

- A referral is made so that the client can access the care identified by the primary care provider or the consultant.

- The care may be provided in the inpatient setting (e.g., physical therapy, occupational therapy) or outside the facility (e.g., hospice care, home health aide).

- Clients being released from health care facilities and discharged to their home still require nursing care.

- Discharge referrals are based on client needs in relation to actual and potential problems and may enlist the aid of:

  ◊   Social services.

  ◊   Specialized therapists (e.g., physical, occupational, speech).

  ◊   Care providers (e.g., home health nurses, hospice nurse).

- Knowledge of community resources is necessary to appropriately link the client with needed services.

Δ   **Collaboration with the Interdisciplinary Team**

- An interdisciplinary team is a group of health care professionals from different disciplines.

- Collaboration is used by interdisciplinary teams to make health care decisions about clients with multiple problems. Collaboration, which may take place at team meetings, allows the achievement of results that the participants would be incapable of accomplishing if working alone.

- Key elements of collaboration include:

  ◊   Effective communication skills.

  ◊   Mutual respect and trust.

  ◊   Shared decision making.

- The nurse contributes:

  ◊   Knowledge of nursing care and its management.

  ◊   A holistic understanding of the client, her health care needs, and health care systems.

- Nurse-primary care provider collaboration should be fostered to create a climate of mutual respect and collaborative practice.

- Collaboration can occur among different levels of nurses and nurses with different areas of expertise.

Nursing Interventions

Δ **Consultations**

- Initiate the necessary consults or notify the primary care provider of the client's needs so the consult can be initiated.

- Provide the consultant with all pertinent information about the problem (e.g., information from the client/family, the client's medical records).

- Incorporate the consultant's recommendations into the client's plan of care.

- Facilitate coordination of the consultant's recommendations with other health care providers' recommendations to protect the client from conflicting and potentially dangerous orders.

Δ **Referrals**

- To ensure continuity of care by the use of referrals, the nurse should:

  ◊ Initiate the discharge plan upon the client's admission.

  ◊ Evaluate client/family competencies in relation to home care prior to discharge.

  ◊ Involve the client and family in care planning.

  ◊ Collaborate with other health care professionals to ensure all health care needs are met.

  ◊ Complete referral forms to ensure proper reimbursement for services ordered.

Δ **Collaboration with the Interdisciplinary Team**

- Use effective communication skills.

- Participate in client rounds and interdisciplinary team meetings.

- Present information relevant to the client's health status and treatment regimen.

- Attend interdisciplinary clinical conferences/case presentations.

Primary Reference:

Marquis, B. L., & Huston, C. J. (2006). *Leadership roles and management functions in nursing: Theory and application* (5th ed.). Philadelphia: Lippincott Williams & Wilkins.

Additional Resources:

Kozier, B., Erb, G., Berman, A., & Snyder, S. (2004). *Fundamentals of nursing: Concepts, process, and practice* (7th ed.). Upper Saddle River, NJ: Prentice Hall.

Chapter 12: Referrals, Consultations, and Collaboration with the Interdisciplinary Team

Application Exercises

1. True or False: Clients remain in the health care facility until they no longer need nursing care.

2. True or False: One reason for client referral is that families may not be able to provide necessary care in the home.

3. Proper completion of discharge summaries when clients are transferred from one facility to another can facilitate _____.

4. A nurse working on a rehabilitation unit attends an interdisciplinary team meeting. Her client, who experienced a cervical spinal cord injury in an automobile accident, will be discussed. What members of the interdisciplinary team should the nurse expect to be involved in developing the client's goals and plan of care?

5. An older adult client is being prepared for discharge to her home with her husband, who is no longer able to drive. The client is 10 days postoperative a below-the-knee amputation of the right leg. She requires insulin to manage diabetes and an ACE inhibitor to manage hypertension. In anticipation of the client's discharge, what referrals should the nurse facilitate?

6. A nurse is assigned to care for an older adult client who has been in the health care facility for 3 weeks due to a total hip replacement and subsequent pulmonary complications. During morning assessment, the nurse notes that the client is beginning to develop a decubitus ulcer on his coccyx. Which of the following actions by the nurse would be most appropriate in an effort to obtain a plan of care for this problem?

      A. Notify the unit manager that staff may not be consistently or effectively carrying out the skin care protocol for high-risk clients.

      B. Call for a consult with the wound care nurse.

      C. Bring the problem to the attention of the surgeon during rounds.

      D. Develop a nursing care plan for "impaired skin integrity: decubitus ulcer."

7. Which of the following support interdisciplinary decision making? (Select all that apply.)

     _____ Open communication and collaboration between team members

     _____ Appreciation of the knowledge and skill each discipline has to offer

     _____ Designation of a nurse who will serve as group facilitator

     _____ Involvement of the client and family

     _____ Submission of consult information by fax

Chapter 12: Referrals, Consultations, and Collaboration with the Interdisciplinary Team

Application Exercises Answer Key

1. True or False: Clients remain in the health care facility until they no longer need nursing care.

   False: Clients being discharged to home still require nursing care.

2. True or False: One reason for client referral is that families may not be able to provide necessary care in the home.

   True: Clients may be discharged to home requiring complex nursing care (e.g., dressing changes, enteral feedings).

3. Proper completion of discharge summaries when clients are transferred from one facility to another can facilitate _____.

   continuity of care

4. A nurse working on a rehabilitation unit attends an interdisciplinary team meeting. Her client, who experienced a cervical spinal cord injury in an automobile accident, will be discussed. What members of the interdisciplinary team should the nurse expect to be involved in developing the client's goals and plan of care?

   Since cervical injuries cause extremely devastating functional deficits, the interdisciplinary team will most likely consist of nurses, medical doctors, physical and occupational therapists, a social worker, a vocational counselor, and a psychologist. The client and family should also be included because they will be affected by decisions made.

5. An older adult client is being prepared for discharge to her home with her husband, who is no longer able to drive. The client is 10 days postoperative a below-the-knee amputation of the right leg. She requires insulin to manage diabetes and an ACE inhibitor to manage hypertension. In anticipation of the client's discharge, what referrals should the nurse facilitate?

   A referral to physical therapy to determine what equipment will be needed in the home and to provide therapy in the home
   A referral to the social worker to assist with obtaining the necessary equipment and subsequent payment
   A referral to home health to provide for immediate needs (e.g., perform dressing changes, monitor blood glucose and blood pressure) and to evaluate the home situation and what support the client will need (e.g., transportation to medical appointments, shopping for medications and supplies)

6. A nurse is assigned to care for an older adult client who has been in the health care facility for 3 weeks due to a total hip replacement and subsequent pulmonary complications. During morning assessment, the nurse notes that the client is beginning to develop a decubitus ulcer on his coccyx. Which of the following actions by the nurse would be most appropriate in an effort to obtain a plan of care for this problem?

    A. Notify the unit manager that staff may not be consistently or effectively carrying out the skin care protocol for high-risk clients.

    B. Call for a consult with the wound care nurse.

    C. Bring the problem to the attention of the surgeon during rounds.

    D. Develop a nursing care plan for "impaired skin integrity: decubitus ulcer."

The nurse should call the wound care nurse for a consult with this client. Since the wound care nurse is an expert in this area, she would be the most knowledgeable person to enlist in the development of a plan of care. While the surgeon should be notified of the decubitus ulcer, she may not be as knowledgeable about treatment options. It is appropriate to notify the unit manager that a client on the unit has developed a decubitus ulcer and that this may indicate a staff education need. However, this action would not facilitate the development of a plan of care for this client. Development of a nursing care plan for "impaired skin integrity: decubitus ulcer" is indicated but should be done with the wound care nurse to enhance the quality of care prescribed.

7. Which of the following support interdisciplinary decision making? (Select all that apply.)

    __X__ **Open communication and collaboration between team members**

    __X__ **Appreciation of the knowledge and skill each discipline has to offer**

    _____ Designation of a nurse who will serve as group facilitator

    __X__ **Involvement of the client and family**

    _____ Submission of consult information by fax

Open communication and appreciation of the knowledge and skill of each discipline is critical for interdisciplinary decision making. Equal contributions by all members are necessary. When appropriate, the client and family should be included in the decision-making process. A nurse does not need to be the facilitator of an interdisciplinary team. The facilitator can be any member of the team involved in the client's care. Submission of information by fax without the presence of the health care provider who made the recommendation does not lend itself to open discussion and collaborative decision making.

Unit 4   Collaborator/Planner of Client Care

Chapter 13:   Continuity of Care, Case Management, and Discharge Planning
Contributor: Annette C. Milius, MA, RN, APRN-BC

 NCLEX® Connections:

Learning Objective: Review and apply knowledge within "**Continuity of Care, Case Management, and Discharge Planning**" in readiness for performance of the following nursing activities as outlined by the NCLEX® test plans:

Δ   Plan and coordinate care of the client based upon the client's needs through all phases of care (admission, transfers, discharge, post-discharge).

Δ   Continuously review and revise the client's care plan as needed.

Δ   Appropriately document and report client information (change-of-shift report) in order to maintain continuity of care.

Δ   Serve as needed as the care coordinator (liaison) between the client and members of the health care team.

Δ   Use clinical pathways and/or care plans to initiate, direct, review, and evaluate client care.

Δ   Ensure continuity of care within the health care facility and with other health care facilities. Investigate resources for the client and family to assist with achievement and maintenance of independence and make referrals as appropriate.

Δ   Prepare the client for discharge to home, hospice, or community setting.

Key Points

Δ   **Continuity of Care**

- Continuity of care is required as clients move through the health care system from one:
    ◊   Level of care to another, such as from a medical unit to the ICU.
    ◊   Facility to another, such as from an acute care facility to a skilled facility.
    ◊   Unit to another, such as from the operating room to the PACU.

- The nurse's role as **care coordinator** is to:

  ◊ Be responsible for facilitating continuity of care.

  ◊ Act as a representative of the client and as a **liaison** when collaborating with other members of the health care team. When acting as a liaison, the nurse is usually serving as a client advocate.

- Coordination of the client's clinical care requires:

The ability to:	The responsibility for:
• Make clinical decisions. • Set priorities. • Organize care and provision of that care. • Manage time efficiently. • Delegate as appropriate. • Evaluate client care outcomes. • Communicate effectively and knowledgeably with all members of the health care team. • Make referrals to available resources.	• Admission, transfer, discharge, and post-discharge orders. • Initiation, revision, and evaluation of the plan of care. • Reporting the client's status to other nurses and the primary care provider. • Coordinating the discharge plan. • Facilitating referrals and the utilization of community resources.

- **Documentation** to facilitate continuity of care includes:

  ◊ Graphic records to illustrate trending of assessment data such as vital signs.

  ◊ Flow sheets to reflect routine care completed and other care-related data.

  ◊ Nurses' notes to describe changes in client status or unusual circumstances.

  ◊ Client care summaries, or Kardexes, to serve as quick references for client care information.

  ◊ Nursing care plans to set the standard for care provided.

    ° Standardized nursing care plans provide a starting point for the nurse responsible for care plan development.

    ° Standardized plans must be individualized to each client.

    ° All documentation should reflect the plan of care.

- **Communication** and Continuity of Care

  ◊ Change-of-shift report

    ° Done either on a one-to-one basis or with an audiotape machine.

    ° Describes the current health status of the client.

    ° Informs the next shift of pertinent client care information.

    ° Provides the oncoming nurse the opportunity to ask questions and clarify the plan of care.

    ° Should be given in a private area, such as a conference room, to protect client confidentiality.

◊ Reports to the primary care provider

  ° Assessment data integral to changes in client status

  ° Recommendations for changes in the interdisciplinary plan of care

  ° Clarification of questionable orders

Δ Case Management

- The Case Management Society of America describes case management as collaboration that assesses, plans, implements, coordinates, monitors, and evaluates the options and services required to meet an individual's health needs, using communications and available resources to promote quality, cost-effective outcomes.

- A case manager is a nurse who coordinates and links health care services provided by the interdisciplinary team to the client and family.

- This nurse does not provide direct client care. Her role is to supervise care and facilitate collaboration between members of the health care team as needed.

- A case manager usually oversees a caseload of clients with similar disorders or treatment regimens.

- A critical pathway or case map may be used as a plan for all interdisciplinary members of the care team to follow.

Δ Discharge Planning

- The process begins at the time of admission.

- Plans are developed with client and family input, focusing on active participation by the client to facilitate a timely discharge.

- Serves as a starting point for continuity of care for the client by the caregiver, home health nurse, or receiving facility.

- The need for additional client or family support is included with recommendations for support services such as home health, outpatient therapy, and respite care.

- Discharge summary includes:

  ◊ Step-by-step instructions for procedures to be done at home.

  ◊ Precautions to take when performing procedures or administering medications.

  ◊ Signs and symptoms of complications that should be reported.

  ◊ Names and numbers of health care providers and community services the client/family can contact.

  ◊ Plans for follow-up care and therapies.

  ◊ Time of discharge, mode of transportation, and who accompanied the client.

Nursing Interventions

Δ   The nurse's role as **care coordinator** includes:

- Coordination of the client's care to provide continuity of care.

- Facilitating communication between the client and the primary care provider.

- Clarifying information given by the primary care provider to the client. Confusing and complex information combined with use of medical jargon may make it hard for the client to understand proposed therapeutic interventions.

- Assisting the client to resolve any conflicts with the primary care provider.

Δ   The nurse's role as **case manager** includes:

- Coordination of care, particularly for clients with complex health care needs.

- Facilitating continuity of care.

- Improving efficiency of care and utilization of resources.

- Enhancing quality of care provided.

- Limiting unnecessary costs and lengthy stays.

- Advocating for the client and family.

Primary Reference:

Marquis, B. L., & Huston, C. J. (2006). *Leadership roles and management functions in nursing: Theory and application* (5th ed.). Philadelphia: Lippincott Williams & Wilkins.

Additional Resources:

Potter, P. A., & Perry, A. G. (2005). *Fundamentals of nursing* (6th ed.). St. Louis, MO: Mosby.

For information on the Case Management Society of America, visit the CMSA Web site, *www.cmsa.org*.

Chapter 13: Continuity of Care, Case Management, and Discharge Planning

Application Exercises

1. True or False: The role of a nursing case manager is to coordinate the care of a small caseload of clients for whose care she is directly responsible.

2. A nurse is preparing to discharge a client from a health care facility to the skilled nursing unit of a long-term care facility. The client experienced a left-sided cardiovascular accident and has right-sided paralysis. She has been receiving physical, occupational, and speech therapy and has had problems with incontinence. What information should the nurse make sure is included in the discharge summary even if he is not directly responsible for supplying the information?

3. Match each of the following documentation tools with the role it plays in providing continuity of care.

_____ Nurses' notes

_____ Graphic record

_____ Flow sheet

_____ Kardex

_____ Nursing care plan

A. Lists routine care to be completed and provides a graph upon which to document care completed.

B. Maintains record of client's response to treatments as well as changes in client status.

C. Provides current and retrospective listing of vital signs.

D. Describes treatment plan and intended outcomes of care.

E. Provides quick reference for client information, a list of treatments and scheduled times, upcoming diagnostic procedures, and special needs.

4. A nurse is preparing to give a change-of-shift report regarding a client with a complex dressing change that is done every shift. The oncoming nurse has not cared for this client before. The oncoming nurse would like to see the client's dressing and asks if the nurse would provide report in the client's room. Which of the following responses by the nurse preparing to leave is most appropriate?

    A. "Sure, just let me pick up the client's chart so I can give you report while we are in there and we can look at the procedure for changing the dressing, too."

    B. "Due to HIPAA regulations, we cannot discuss client information in the room so I will do my best to describe the dressing and how to change it during report in the conference room."

    C. "Let me give you report in the conference room first, and then we can visit the client and I will show you the dressing and how I have been changing it."

    D. "The orders for the dressing change are provided in detail on the Kardex. You should be able to change the dressing without difficulty if you follow them."

5. The name of the tool that is used by various members of the health care team to direct and focus their care is a _____.

6. Which of the following skills are necessary for a nurse to be able to fulfill the role of a care coordinator? (Select all that apply.)

    _____ Good communication skills

    _____ Understanding of the nursing process

    _____ Knowledge of community resources

    _____ Good delegation skills

    _____ Expertise in all fields of nursing

Chapter 13: Continuity of Care, Case Management, and Discharge Planning

Application Exercises Answer Key

1. True or False: The role of a nursing case manager is to coordinate the care of a small caseload of clients for whose care she is directly responsible.

   False: The nurse case manager does not provide direct client care. She is responsible for coordinating the efforts of the interdisciplinary team while containing costs of care and decreasing length of stay. The description above refers to the role of the nurse as care coordinator or primary care nurse.

2. A nurse is preparing to discharge a client from a health care facility to the skilled nursing unit of a long-term care facility. The client experienced a left-sided cardiovascular accident and has right-sided paralysis. She has been receiving physical, occupational, and speech therapy and has had problems with incontinence. What information should the nurse make sure is included in the discharge summary even if he is not directly responsible for supplying the information?

   The discharge summary should include:

   History of current illness, other coexisting illnesses.
   Current level of functional abilities, perhaps in the form of a functional assessment tool.
   Medical orders from the primary care provider for medications and treatments.
   A summary of physical, occupational, and speech therapy provided and current goals.
   Description of bladder and bowel program instituted and client or family education that has been provided.
   Status of client upon discharge, mode of transportation, and who accompanied the client.

3. Match each of the following documentation tools with the role it plays in providing continuity of care.

B Nurses' notes

C Graphic record

A Flow sheet

E Kardex

D Nursing care plan

A. Lists routine care to be completed and provides a graph upon which to document care completed.

B. Maintains record of client's response to treatments as well as changes in client status.

C. Provides current and retrospective listing of vital signs.

D. Describes treatment plan and intended outcomes of care.

E. Provides quick reference for client information, a list of treatments and scheduled times, upcoming diagnostic procedures, and special needs.

4. A nurse is preparing to give a change-of-shift report regarding a client with a complex dressing change that is done every shift. The oncoming nurse has not cared for this client before. The oncoming nurse would like to see the client's dressing and asks if the nurse would provide report in the client's room. Which of the following responses by the nurse preparing to leave is most appropriate?

    A. "Sure, just let me pick up the client's chart so I can give you report while we are in there and we can look at the procedure for changing the dressing, too."

    B. "Due to HIPAA regulations, we cannot discuss client information in the room so I will do my best to describe the dressing and how to change it during report in the conference room."

    C. "Let me give you report in the conference room first, and then we can visit the client and I will show you the dressing and how I have been changing it."

    D. "The orders for the dressing change are provided in detail on the Kardex. You should be able to change the dressing without difficulty if you follow them."

Due to HIPAA regulations, nurses can no longer give report in or just outside the client's room. Report should be given in a private location with a door, such as a conference room. Since the dressing change is complex, it is the responsibility of the nurse who is leaving to ensure that the oncoming nurse provides continuity of care by correctly performing the dressing change on her shift. This can be done after report by going into the room and quietly discussing only this facet of client care. Even though the orders for the dressing change are on the Kardex, the oncoming nurse has verbalized she is unsure of how to do it, so additional information and demonstration should be provided.

5. The name of the tool that is used by various members of the health care team to direct and focus their care is a _____.

critical pathway or case map

6. Which of the following skills are necessary for a nurse to be able to fulfill the role of a care coordinator? (Select all that apply.)

   X   Good communication skills
   X   Understanding of the nursing process
   X   Knowledge of community resources
   X   Good delegation skills
   _____ Expertise in all fields of nursing

One of the most important skills for a nurse to possess in relation to continuity of client care is communication. The nurse as care coordinator will find it necessary to communicate with various levels of nurses, the client and family, and other members of the health care team. Knowledge of the nursing process is necessary to develop an individualized plan of care that can be shared with other nurses. Good delegation skills will enable the nurse to obtain assistance as appropriate. When a client is facing discharge and will need additional care, information about community resources that can help with this care should be provided. The nurse does not need expertise in all fields of nursing to be able to provide continuity of care for clients.